HOLLYWOOD SISTERS:
JACKIE AND JOAN COLLINS

HOLLYWOOD SISTERS: JACKIE AND JOAN COLLINS

Susan Crimp and Patricia Burstein

 Robson Books

First published in Great Britain in 1989 by Robson Books Ltd, Bolsover House, 5-6 Clipstone Street, London W1P 7EB

Copyright © 1988 Susan Crimp and Patricia Burstein

British Library Cataloguing in Publication Data

Crimp, Susan
 Hollywood sisters: the story of Jackie and Joan Collins.
 1. Cinema films. Acting. Collins, Joan, 1933 –
 Biographies.
 2. Fiction in English. Collins, Jackie.
 I. Title II. Burstein, Patricia.
 791.43'028'0924.

ISBN 0 86051 584 2

Printed in Great Britain by St Edmundsbury Press Limited, Bury St Edmunds, Suffolk.

FOR NANNA WITH ALL MY LOVE and to my friends and family, especially Daddy, John Edward Crimp; my uncle, Frederick V. Crimp; and my brother, Steven John Spencer Crimp . . . and John-John always.

Susan Crimp

With love to my sisters Ellen, Karen and Jessica; and John and Judd; and above all, my late father, Herbert Burstein, Esquire, and my mother, Justice Beatrice S. Burstein.

Patricia Burstein

Contents

ACKNOWLEDGMENTS

The authors would like to thank the following people: Barbara Cartland; Gerald Harper; Tony Hall; Douglas Hayward; Juliet Simpkins of Madame Tussaud's in London; Pearly Queen Pat Hannam, Clerical Officer/Nurse, Central Middlesex Hospital, London; Maureen Simmons, Old Girls' Association, Francis Holland School; Kenneth O'Donoghue, Royal Academy of Dramatic Art; Barry Greenwood-Smith; and, our editor, Charles E. Spicer, and his assistant, Bill Thomas, for their help.

REFERENCES

Material for this book was gathered in personal interviews, and additional information taken from the following sources:

The New York Times
The Washington Post
The *New York Post*
The Daily News, New York
Sunday Mirror, England
Options Magazine, England
Today newspaper, England
US magazine
People magazine
Los Angeles Herald Examiner
The *Sun*, England
The Sunday Express, England
The Guardian, England
Parade magazine
GQ magazine
U.S.A. Today
Time magazine

Books:
Past Imperfect: An Autobiography, by Joan Collins
A Biography, Joan Collins, by Robert Levine
A Touch of Collins, by Joe Collins
TV Babylon, by Jeff Rovin

Introduction

They are the ultimate immigrant success story. And next to the steamy Hollywood Sisters, Jackie and Joan Collins, even the tales of Hollywood wives, husbands, and kids seem tepid. The story of the two immigrant sisters is the stuff miniseries are made of. The sisters from Maida Vale, London, migrate to Los Angeles, and Tinsel Town, always poised for an earthquake, definitely feels the tremors. Alternately vamping and camping it up, they manage almost simultaneously to both terrorize and titillate the town. Jackie is the wicked authoress, chronicling the sexual acrobatics of the international jet set while Joan plays the part of the beauteous TV-bitch Alexis who schemes for sex and money. Jackie writes the scenes and Joan acts them.

Behind the pages or in front of the camera, Jackie and Joan Collins are household names. Jackie's twelve novels have sold over seventy million copies in many countries. And her latest book contract, Jackie quipped, is worth an amount somewhere in the region of the Brazilian national debt. Meanwhile, Joan, in her Alexis incarnation, slinks across television screens all over the globe. Joan Collins also comes in wax. (At Madame Tussaud's in London, Joan is the conservatory's waxwork centerpiece.) She has also had her own line of perfume, lingerie, blouses, hats, fake jewelry, designer jeans, home videos, and posters. And there is hardly a major book outlet without a Jackie Collins novel dominating the racks and out-selling most of the competition.

Miniseries are also part of the Hollywood Sis-ters' winning formula. Jackie's novels, most nota-bly *Hollywood Wives*, inspire them, and Joan has also produced and starred in *Sins* and *Monte Carlo*. These are the same sisters who put out the movies *The Stud* and *The Bitch*. Jackie wrote them, and Joan played the tarty disco doyenne Fontaine in both. The role rescued Joan from her walk-on part at the unemployment office in Santa Monica and worldwide obscurity and, more importantly, led to her role as Alexis on *Dynasty*, catapulting her to worldwide celebrity.

Who are these remarkable sisters? How did they emerge as among the most popular exports from Britain, better known for its Rolls Royce and Royal Family? While most middle-class families, like the one they came from, make do with one doctor and one lawyer, the Collins family boasts two mega-stars. What's more, the two sisters achieved their enormous celebrity in another country, more than three thousand miles and an ocean away from their native England.

Determination, drive, and talent characterize the Hollywood Sisters as much as glitz and glamour. From the time they were little, they struggled to assert themselves with their father, a theatrical agent, whose controlling ways seemed suffocating at times. Much as they loved and cherished their mother, they vowed that they would never allow themselves to be cast, like her, in the role of sub-missive wife.

The Hollywood Sisters fashioned their own lives. Jackie invented a fictional world while Joan made-believe on stage and screen. At times, though, Joan has given new meaning to the notion that fact can be stranger than fiction. Witness her divorce from her fourth husband, Swedish rocker Peter Holm. It reads like a page from one of Jackie's ribald novels.

The Hollywood Sisters are survivors. They can take the knocks with the kudos. "With both Jackie and Joan," says a male friend of both, "you are aware that you are in the presence of two formidable persons." Armed with wit, Jackie pokes fun at herself before interviewers can take aim. Joan, once perilously close to becoming a pathetic party joke, proves that there *are* second acts in America. Against all odds, Joan, not getting any younger and not getting any offers of roles, resurrected herself as a major star and sex symbol. Then, at fifty, she risked public ridicule by posing for *Playboy* in what would become a sellout issue and collector's item. In so doing, she succeeded in breaking the ageism taboo. Jackie, meanwhile, instructs through her characters that women can triumph over Svengali types, deceiving husbands, and even the "stud," who is sexually exploited by women and then tossed out on his proverbial derrière.

Both sisters have forged their own identities. Though Jackie started out, albeit reluctantly, as an actress, she is adamant about defining herself solely as a writer. Long ago she demanded that the label "ex-actress" be removed from the jackets of her novels. "If you blinked," Jackie the writer jokes, "you missed my acting career." Clearly, she prefers it this way. Joan has made some forays into the writing field, until *Prime Time* secondary to her acting career. There was the almost obligatory beauty book and tell-all autobiography. A third was a personal account of how, through unwavering love and support, she healed her daughter after a near-fatal accident. The title of the book was *Katy*. At the time of Joan's autobiography *Past Im-*

perfect (1978), a London editor remembers asking her about writing a novel. To which, he says, Joan responded: "Well, Jackie has got the real talent in writing fiction." Joan concentrated instead on acting. Her choice paid off. *Dynasty* came next. Nonetheless, her autobiography became a best-seller.

Today, Joan finds the role of writer most appealing and hints this season may be her last on *Dynasty*. Joan's first novel, *Prime Time*, about five actresses competing for the same soap-opera role, made the best-seller lists in America and Britain. And she has already started writing her second novel. Jackie, meanwhile, continues to turn out one best-seller after the other. Rumors of sibling rivalry surface regularly in the press.

Though their professional paths are now beginning to cross, their private lives remain distinctly different. Jackie has been married to the same man for over twenty years, while Joan recently divorced her fourth husband. They both have three children. Jackie prefers to stay home; Joan likes to go out. Jackie, in her trademark jungle-pattern outfits, hasn't worn a dress in years, while Joan favors designer gowns. Both sisters, though, know how to apply the makeup. Jackie does not like to travel by air. Joan is a British Airways Concorde Frequent Flier. Jackie is at home in America. Joan gets homesick for England and her villa in the South of France. Jackie, except for book promotion tours, eschews the limelight. Joan, clearly, covets it.

What are these Hollywood Sisters really like? And what will the next chapter in their careers bring? Is a "Battle of the Best-sellers" looming? Stay tuned—or better yet—keep reading.

Kid Sisters

Almost from the moment of birth, Joan Henrietta Collins got mixed reviews. She arrived at 7 A.M. on May 23, 1933, at a nursing home in Bayswater, near London's Hyde Park. At first sight of the baby, nestled in her mother's warm and loving arms, her father remarked, "What's that bit of scrag you've got there?" Any pampering was left to her mother who, believing that Joan was irresistibly adorable, fixed a sign to her pram. "Please do not kiss me," the sign read, warding off potential purveyors of germs.

Throughout her childhood Joan got polar responses from her parents. "I had a very strict father," she says, "and a very loving mother." In appearance and background her parents were also worlds apart. Joe Collins, with his jet-black, curly hair, sprang from a line of Jewish businessmen who were fishmongers, ice-cream vendors, and vaudeville impresarios. Elsa Collins, blond and blue-eyed, was a Protestant. Of his decision to marry Elsa Bessant, a dance instructor and one of eleven children of a tram driver, Joe Collins explains in his autobiography: "She was just right: three years younger than me, home-loving, very feminine, and she certainly would not develop into the aggressive type of woman who might try to interfere in my show-business life." By then Joe Collins was starting his career as a theatrical agent and entrepreneur, eventually representing, among others, Peter Sellers, Shirley Bassey, and Roger Moore in the early stages of their careers.

Throughout both Joan and Jackie's childhood, their father would play the dominant role, often drowning out everyone with his hollering, while their mother cushioned his verbal assaults with an unequivocating, gentle affection for the daughters. She would even heat ice cream for the infant Joan so it would not be cold to the taste. Joe exerted his influence even in the choice of names for his children. Joan, according to her father, was a feminization of Joseph. The middle name given to her was Henrietta after Joe's mother. Joe kept things alliterative by naming his second daughter Jacqueline Jill, calling her, as if in nursery rhyme, "Jackie Jill." Later on it was just "Jack," even to boyfriends. The girls' baby brother William also got his name from the Collins side. Their grandfather was Will Collins, a successful vaudeville impresario who had changed his name from Isaac Hart out of devotion to his favorite music-hall star, Lottie Collins.

Show business was in Joan's blood. Further, as the first-born child, she occupied the privileged position of center stage. The show-business legacy of the Collins family passed most directly to her. There was grandmother Henrietta, affectionately known as Hettie, who was a musical-comedy star in South Africa prior to marrying and moving back to England. Joan's paternal aunts, Lalla and Pauline, also knew how to kick up their heels on London's West End stage during the Roaring Twenties. Lalla, the older one, even made it to Broadway in a revue. Pauline swathed herself in white furs and sipped champagne for breakfast.

Unlike Joan, who carried on with her career throughout her four marriages and child-bearing years, her aunts eventually bowed out of the stage.

One gave it up upon marrying; and the other switched to the business side in her mid-thirties. But it was largely through them, as well as Grandma Hettie, that Joan became infused with dreams of stardom. Apparently she also inherited their genes. Both aunts always looked far younger than their years. And Joan's grandmother Hettie, at seventy, could still do the splits. Joan copied Hettie's hip-swaying walk, and at her side learned dance steps and acrobatics. Hettie also taught Joan how to make her eyelashes stronger and longer by balancing matchsticks on them. At six years of age, Joan got, as a present from Hettie, a white rabbit-fur coat and a vanity bag. By then, Joan had already developed a penchant for wearing pretty dresses with a matching bow in her hair.

Joan saw a great deal of these relatives while growing up. Most Sundays, her parents would take Joan to visit her grandmother in Brighton, a seaside town with white Regency-style buildings about fifty miles south of London. Joe owned a car in those days. The Collins family was comfortably middle class. In money matters, Joe was also in the driver's seat. Joan's mother had to save out of her housekeeping coffers or use her powers of persuasion for little extras.

Joan's early dreams of stardom were inextricably bound with her need for financial independence. "I vowed at an early age," she says in her autobiography, *Past Imperfect,* "that my desires for material things would never depend on the whims of a man. It was extremely important to me to become financially independent as soon as possible." In a curious role reversal, Joan would become the provider for husbands, boyfriends, and children. In order to shed the doormat role that seemed to belong to her mother, Joan had to act out the part of her father as controller of the purse strings.

Both daughters resented their father's chauvinism. But Joan seemed to dwell on this while Jackie distanced herself from it. Up until her father's death in April of 1988, Joan kept coming back for his approval. Jackie, with her writer's sensibility, seemed more the detached observer. Even as a child she could silence her father's rantings by retreating to her room for hours on end and living inside her imagination.

Yet Joan was as much a survivor as Jackie. In her first year, she escaped a fire that would have snuffed out her life in their Maida Vale, North London, home. Baby Joan, cutting her teeth, was to remain behind while her parents went on their Sunday drive to visit Joe's mother. But on this particular day Joan's squealing convinced them to take her along. The Collins family returned to find their house burned down to the ground. Joan's young live-in babysitter, who had the day off, said that she might have dropped a lighted cigarette before leaving the house that day. In the aftermath of the fire, a neighbor took the family in until they could find new lodgings.

If Joan's childhood was colored to a large extent by her father's domineering ways, it was also cushioned and propped up by the way her mother and relatives doted on her. For the first eight years of her life, she was the only grandchild. True to her Gemini nature, Joan was a moody child, incredibly charming one moment and slightly impossible the next. Always, she was on stage. Her father remembers her sashaying around a room, hand on hip, declaring, "I'm a lady going to a ball."

Just as Joan was getting used to being the belle of the ball around the Collins household, along came baby sister Jackie to share the spotlight. The first chapter of Jackie's life began on October 4, 1941. Both sisters subscribe to the Oscar Wilde theory: "Any woman who would reveal her age would reveal anything." Jackie comments wryly: "That means I'm eight years younger than whatever age Joan is telling the magazines she is that week." Those eight years, however, would make a huge difference. Jackie would be born into a world that was far less secure than Joan's. Hitler was advancing across Europe. Maybe due to an unconscious awareness of what was happening around her, Jackie was from the beginning a very sensitive child. Her senses, as well, seemed to be heightened. On Sunday outings to visit the girls' grandmother, Jackie hated the smell of the leather upholstery in her father's car. Often she rode in silence on these trips to Brighton. Jackie would not spend as much time as Joan with her grandmother because of the war.

While Joan worshipped their father, Jackie was by all accounts closer to their mother. During the war years, when Elsa and the daughters were evacuated from London, Jackie saw little of her father who stayed behind to work, visiting them on weekends. Nonetheless Jackie did not escape Joe's harsh criticisms throughout her childhood. "When I was a small girl," she remembers, "and I asked him a question, he'd say, 'You're old enough and ugly enough to know.' The word ugly was demeaning, but that's what made me want to succeed. I had to prove I wasn't ugly and that I could do anything I set my mind to do." She adds: "My father was a bit of a male chauvinist to say the least. I grew up thinking 'Why do men always come first? It's ridiculous.'" For Joan, his absence was as compelling as his presence. She missed her father much of the time. Joan, then eight, was, according to her father, alarmed, but confused about what was actually happening. "Are you sending us away, Daddy?"

her father remembers Joan asking in plaintive tones. "Why are you doing it?"

For the next six years the London Blitz formed the backdrop of their lives. They lived outside of London much of the time. But with any lull in the bombing, Joe would bring them back to the city only to see the raids start again. They lived at one point with relatives who had an air-raid shelter in the basement of their apartment near London's Marble Arch. By day Joe and Elsa would go back to their own flat.

One morning they found it had been blown to pieces by an explosion of bombs the previous night. No trace was left of Joan and Jackie's bedroom in the house that had been sliced in half. "By now Joan was so scared," her father recalls, "that she had to sleep with the light on."

Worried that his daughters would grow up to be nervous wrecks, Joe Collins moved the family still again, this time to a hilly seaside resort in North Devon, some two hundred miles from London, near their aunt Lalla, and her husband. Owing to the distance, Joe only visited them once every two weeks. On one such visit Joe took Joan to see a beached enemy aircraft and also showed her a bayonet stained with blood. The latter, according to her father, made an indelible impression on Joan.

During the war years their schooling was as unsettled as their living arrangements. In total, according to Joan's own calculation, she had attended thirteen schools by the time she reached her teens. One of them was in the tiny hillside town of Ilfracombe, a hilly resort town on the Bristol Channel. There she did well at drama, English, and art. As soon as Jackie could read and write— though she would never win a spelling contest— she proved to be a natural-born storyteller. Jackie made up stories to go with Joan's drawings.

With the war ended, in 1945, Joan, then twelve, and Jackie, four, were brought back to London. They moved first to a rented flat on Portland Street before settling into Harley House on Marylebone Road. It was Harley House, where Joe Collins remained until 1975, that the daughters would regard as their childhood home. Once a monastery, Harley House is a landmark building today. Architecturally, its style is late Victorian, with a portland stone balcony. In its heyday Harley House was quite grand, but now, in need of a washing, it has a gray-green pallor that makes the place look haunted. Inside, the reception area is graced with handcrafted wood and fireplaces. In the days Joan and Jackie were growing up there, Harley House housed the offices and clinics of many doctors in the Harley Street district of London. In later years it attracted the managers of rock stars like Eric Clapton and groups such as Genesis. Mick Jagger also resided there until, according to a building employee, he carved his initials in a lobby fireplace and practically ripped up the place.

The Collins family lived in apartment No. 15, one of the hundred flats there. It was in the basement, but quite rambling, with a large reception area. Their backyard was a concrete block, but Regent's Park with acres of grass was just around the corner. Out front, a Christmas tree the girls' father planted some years ago is part of the shrubbery.

In those days the rent came to about $1,000 a year, as compared with $40,000 today. Still, in those days one had to be quite well off to afford the rent. If the basement flat was empty of sunlight, it was brightened considerably by the warmth of their mother's hospitality. Nights, they were exposed to famous people, clients of their father and other agents, who often came around for card games. Occasionally, even the building porter was invited to join Joe for a drink there. The tenor of the home, set by their father, tended to be more booker, as in theatrical agent, than bookish.

Joan was more outgoing than Jackie, who would stay alone in her room and read. Joan was more fixated on dressing up and looking pretty while Jackie could be just as easily engaged by the train set and model cars of her younger brother. Their baby brother, William Richard, was born soon after the war, on May 1, 1946. While growing up, Jackie seemed more drawn to her baby brother than her big sister. In part, it may have been that they were closer in age, only five years apart. More likely it was a question of temperament. Jackie and Bill had a special bond. They were both more private and shy than Joan. Enormously protective of her brother, Jackie even had him along on summer strolls through nearby Regent's Park with a boyfriend when she was in her late teens. Much like Jackie, who avoids publicity except to promote her books, Bill, a successful businessman today, rarely gives any interviews about his famous older sisters.

Despite her discomfort around her father, Jackie extended herself here as well by accompanying him to football games. These outings provided Joe Collins with lasting memories: "Jackie came with me to football games more often than the others and made a genuine effort to share my enthusiasm and to understand the mystique and fellowship of being in the crowd cheering on our team." He continues: "She would wear a scarf in the red-and-white Arsenal colors which she had embroidered with the names of the players. For all her efforts, which I appreciated, I realized that at heart she was only doing it to please daddy." Years later that experience would serve her when she wrote a screenplay, *Yesterday's Hero*, about a football player.

Jackie was by all accounts a caring and loving child. Unlike Joan, busy with outside activities, Jackie pitched in willingly. Jackie was, simply, thoughtful. One example was how she cared for her first poodle. Jackie burst into tears when her father started shouting in anger after the dog urinated on the family's prized Chinese rug. "Little Jackie burst into tears and became so upset," he recalls. "She has never forgotten the incident." Later on she stayed up all night to help the same poodle deliver a litter of five puppies.

In childhood, both Joan and Jackie decided on their career paths. In a curious way their mother—though a housewife—was their role model. They never wanted to be controlled, the way she was by their father. For themselves, as much as for their mother, whom they loved deeply, they wanted to run their own lives. Even as an eight-year-old, Joan was determined to become an actress. Joan's debut, at twelve, was a disaster. She was playing a boy in Ibsen's *A Doll's House* at a school that specialized in training children for the theater. It was a small part—she had no lines. "I missed a couple of cues," she recalls, "and I thought it was a bit boring because most of the time I was sitting backstage reading a comic book while waiting to go on." The director took her mistakes more seriously. Furious, he declared, "We will never have children in our plays again."

Jackie felt a strong desire to write. "Ever since I was a kid, I always read Chandler and Fitzgerald," she recalls. "I particularly adored Mickey Spillane." She spent many hours holed up in her room with the latter's books. She preferred to be alone with her books. "I was a loner living out the fantasies of the books I read, like *Truck Stop Girl*, or the movies I saw about fifteen times, like *The Wild One*. Growing up in England I was fascinated by anything American. My ambition was to get to Hollywood to be a writer or a journalist." The girls' interests merged quite successfully when Jackie would write stories and then paste the paper dolls Joan cut out as illustrations.

At eleven, Jackie wrote her first grown-up story, a fantasy about a girl who wants to be a film star. It was a natural enough choice of subject matter since she and Joan were both mad for the movies and had pinups of their favorite stars on their walls. Jackie's favorites were Tony Curtis and Rock Hudson; Joan was sold on British star Maxwell Reed, who would become her first husband when she was only eighteen. Jackie was also hooked on reading. After her father caught her reading D. H. Lawrence's *Lady Chatterley's Lover,* which Jackie had found hidden among his shirts, he exploded in anger. "I'm disgusted with you. That book's pornographic. You must not read books like this." To which Jackie coolly replied, "You're too late, Daddy. I already read it." In no time Jackie graduated to devouring Henry Miller's *Tropic of Cancer,* which she ferreted out of the tool box in her father's car. Joan, meanwhile, discovered *Forever Amber,* which to this day remains "the sexiest book I ever read." She aroused her father's anger by asking him what certain four-letter words in the book meant. She consulted the library instead. But her fascination with smutty words has long since worn off. Today Joan has what she calls a Swear Box in her house. "Ten pence for the *F* word," she says somewhat delicately. "Fifteen pence for the *S* word." Then, wryly, "Roger Moore was over the other day and he was two pounds poorer." Joan adds that her children can say any words they like in school or with friends, but not in front of her.

In his autobiography Joe Collins reflects on the influence of such works on Jackie's own best-selling books today: "Looking back, I wonder now if Jackie learned a useful tip through me; even a non-reader like me will buy a book if everyone is talking about it, saying it's spicy and shocking. Perhaps that is why she chose to write such books herself. I wonder what kind of books Jackie would have written had I kept shelves full of classics." Soon she was inventing all her own characters. Two of them, according to her father, were Lucky Lucy and Roger Rat. (Years later Jackie wrote a best-seller she called *Lucky*.) And, of course, there would be plenty of rats—cheating husbands, deceiving bitches, mobsters—to fill the pages of her novels.

Joan in her own autobiography, *Past Imperfect*, would think twice about those *F* and *S* words on the eve of its United States publication. It was published first in England during a fallow period in her career. It was full of four-letter words. But several years later when Joan, by then on *Dynasty*, was asked to update the book with an extra 110 pages for a paperback edition for America, she deleted a good number of those words. "When she wrote the book," says Bob Tanner, chairman and managing director of the English publishing company, W. H. Allen, "she wanted it to be sensational. I think she wrote it for money. She hadn't got *Dynasty* then. Compare the first and later editions and you'll see the difference."

Despite Joan's more recent forays into writing, as a child she had her heart set on acting. At twelve, she persuaded her parents to let her board at a renowned theatrical school in Hertfordshire. Joe Collins was sufficiently well-off to pay for this. There was always money for a nice flat, pretty clothes for the girls, and even a trip while the girls were still in their teens to the South of France with an aunt. Joe owned at one time a royal-blue Bristol

405 convertible with Mexican tan leather. Still, he was generally more cautious than extravagant in his spending habits.

Joan found boarding school a bit too rugged for her taste. She begged her parents to let her return home on the grounds that she was forced to make her bed, clean her room, and wash her hair with scouring powder. Her mother, who could never do enough for the children, was only too glad to have Joan back. But her father made Joan stay there for a few weeks before bringing her home.

School in general would never be a favorite of either daughter or their brother Bill who went directly into business instead of to a university. There was never any particular push in this direction from either parent. Their father, a self-described nonreader, believes they learned a thing or two about business around the house. "They became exposed to the qualities of a good business agent," Joe Collins boasts. "Drive, foresight and shrewd judgment."

The last exposure to formal education for both girls would be at the Francis Holland School at Clarence Gate, a few blocks away from their Harley House flat. Founded in 1878, it is a Church of England school with a motto from Psalm 144: "That our daughters may be as the polished corners of the temple." Clearly, neither Joan nor Jackie, who attended the school at different times, made a conscious effort to live up to that description. At the time Joan attended Francis Holland, the school was in a sorry state physically. It had been blasted by bombs during the war. The school in fact had been shut down between 1940 and 1945.

Joan was one of the 180 pupils, ranging in age from five to thirteen, who attended the school fairly soon after the war. Though the school had been literally pieced back together, there were still repairs to be done. Thus Joan, along with her classmates, would look up from the schoolbooks and see workmen knocking out the remains of old windows and replacing them with new ones. The sound of pneumatic drills as workmen demolished a concrete air-raid shelter in the playground frequently intruded on the lessons. English, French, and Latin were among the subjects taught there. Daily prayers were said in assembly. On a lighter note, pupils played on the fields of nearby Regent's Park which were so idyllic that the sound of the cuckoo in early spring competed with the rival notes of games whistles.

Occasionally Joan, according to Maureen Simmons, head of the school's Old Girls Association and once secretary to the headmistress, skipped out on her team to go to the movies. Simmons remembers the late headmistress, I. C. Joslin, saying that Joan would have made a very good Shakespearean actress. "The staff certainly liked Joan," Ms. Simmons reports. "She was a clever little girl and a little naughty—but in an amusing way. She put frills on her school uniform." Francis Holland girls wore gray tunics and white blouses with red ties and red-and-white headbands on their gray felt hats.

The school's English mistress, according to Ms. Simmons, thought Joan, not Jackie, was quite good at English composition. The headmistress, who passed away in 1986, attended Joan's first wedding. "She was always intrigued and interested and thoroughly amused by Joan's success," Ms. Simmons remembers. "She always said Joan was an actress."

The high point of Joan's experience at Francis Holland was a school outing to see Laurence Olivier and Ralph Richardson at the Old Vic in Shakespeare's *Henry IV*, Part I. Joan and Jackie would become the most famous Francis Holland School students from that period. Most women either got married or became teachers then. Later on the school produced one of the physicians to the Royal Family and England's first woman rabbi.

Jackie hardly got rave notices. "She was a very ordinary girl," Ms. Simmons recalls, "nondescript, just a sort of ill-mannered, finicky girl, living under the shadow of Joan who had been a clever and charming little girl." The English mistress, she says, cannot remember any instances of Jackie showing any writing talent. That same teacher, curious years later to read one of Jackie's books, reportedly returned the copy of the book in a paper bag to the library.

Jackie stood out in one way. At five feet nine inches, she was a full five inches taller than Joan. Ms. Simmons remembers that Jackie, despite her pigtails, looked older than Joan. By her own admission, Jackie says that she did poorly at Francis Holland. Perhaps her mind was elsewhere. At thirteen, she had already written her first novel, a sort of carbon copy of a Mickey Spillane work. Ever resourceful, Jackie sold peeks at the risqué limericks—" 'Twas on the good ship Venus, my God you should have seen us . . ."—to school chums.

It was around that time that Jackie says that she came into her own. "At thirteen, I seized control of my life. I simply refused to go to school. I played truant. I went to the movies. I forged notes." At fifteen she was thrown out of school. "I was expelled for smoking," she says. "I've made it without education. Actually I'm an eccentric."

Earlier, Joan had also bowed out of school. On her sixteenth birthday she declared her intention to be an actress. Her father tried to dissuade her. "Acting can be very short-lived for a pretty girl unless she's progressed to character parts," her father warned. "You can be famous at 20 and forgotten at 27. You can get very hurt." Joan held her ground on this issue. Her father tried another tactic. He convinced Joan that it was important to study at the Royal Academy of Dramatic Art. Of course, he never thought that she would pass the entrance exam and capture one of the few coveted positions at RADA.

Joan passed with flying colors. In her audition Joan played both Cleopatra in *Antony and Cleopatra* and Emily in *Our Town*. Her first RADA report card read, in part, "Joan has a good personality and a lot of stage presence, but if she doesn't watch her voice projection it will be the films for her and that would be such a pity." The late Sir Kenneth Barnes, RADA's principal, also warned her not to be seduced by press headlines that were already proclaiming her "Britain's best bet since Jean Simmons." At RADA Joan played seductive roles like Jessica in *The Merchant of Venice* and Joanna in *Present Laughter*.

Already some of her RADA classmates were finding her quite seductive. One of them was Gerald Harper, today a British actor and BBC radio host. Of his own decision to become an actor Harper recalls, "I went into the Army to be a doctor and two years later came out a drama student. During my first lesson at RADA there was seventeen-year-old Joan Collins looking truly beautiful, very young, very naïve, in full bloom, and I knew I made the right choice of career." Harper rhapsodizes further: "I thought she was like a beautiful little Labrador puppy, coltish and young." It was during that period that Joan started getting interested in boys. Her interest, according to Harper, was more than duly reciprocated.

Today RADA's general administrator and registrar, Richard O'Donoghue, who in recent years accompanied her on a visit to the school as part of a documentary of her life, says that everyone is mighty proud of Joan. RADA, which spawned actors such as John Gielgud and Trevor Howard, considers Joan among the most famous of all its alumni. "I think her success is so wonderful," O'Donoghue says. "I think there's room for *Oh, Calcutta* at one extreme and Samuel Beckett at the other and in between a whole host of things. She's in the glamour pigeonhole. There's no doubt about that."

During one summer break Joan performed in a repertory theater outside London. There she did everything from small parts to helping backstage and painting scenery. That stint made it possible for Joan's agent father to put a photo of her and a few lines in *Spotlight,* the casting directory. Her repertory work gave her the necessary credentials to get a listing in that publication.

By then Joan was also modeling. She posed for illustrations for love stories in women's magazines, and teen clothes for women in *Woman's Own.* In those days Joan's trademark outfits were a far cry from Nolan Miller's *Dynasty* creations. It was more like jeans, work shirts, and black polo-necked sweaters. Gypsy gold earrings were the basic accessory.

It was only a matter of time before Joan would put the glamour on. And her younger sister Jackie would write about it.

Joan Heads for Hollywood

Draped in her first mink coat, twenty-one-year old Joan still seemed childlike and vulnerable to her parents as they waited with her for her flight to Hollywood. Standing around the airline terminal at London's Heathrow, her father could not hold back his thoughts. If Joe Collins was confident about his daughter's professional future, he did not feel similarly about what might be awaiting her on the personal front. He expressed these misgivings to Joan, who, in turn, gave him some promises. "Daddy, I'm not going to play around in Hollywood the way I sometimes did over here," she assured him. "I'm going to get down to some hard work. I hope they'll give me good parts, not the awful 'Bad Girl' roles. I've had enough of that 'Baby Temptress' label."

Her father had cause for concern. Three years earlier, at eighteen, Joan had made an ill-advised and failed marriage to an Irish-born British actor, Maxwell Reed, who was fourteen years older. That experience, Joan's father believed, had left his daughter shaky and done nothing to enhance her self-image. What of the Hollywood heartthrobs? Would his daughter be so impressionable again?

Her reputation as "Britain's Bad Girl" preceded her arrival in Hollywood. It derived from her sexy delinquent-teen roles. This description did not match her private behavior. The press, smitten with her gorgeous, seductive looks, may have fastened their own longings for a new femme fatale onto Joan. As the now-defunct English paper *Reveille* had proclaimed earlier, "She has the come-hither eyes of Ava Gardner, the sultry look of Lauren Bacall, a Jane Russell figure, and more sex appeal at her age than any other film actress I've met."

Unbeknownst to her public, around the Collins home, Joan was nicknamed Goody Twoshoes by younger sister Jackie who thought she was too much of a prude with men. Jackie arrived at this conclusion from eavesdropping on Joan's telephone conversations. Their father put a stop to this by removing the extension from Jackie's room. If "Temptress" was not the truth about Joan, "Eavesdropper" seemed as apt a description as any for Jackie. It would become a lifetime habit of hers. Later on she would eavesdrop in person—at discos, parties, restaurants, country clubs, beauty salons— on Hollywood wives and husbands, among others, instead of her sister. Eavesdropping would prove to be a profitable exercise, yielding one best-seller after the other.

Joan, no eavesdropper, behaved in a quite exemplary way at home and work. Yet the naughty image persisted in her professional life. Even the first man with whom, as she put it somewhat indelicately, she had "done it" could not quite believe her innocence. "Gorgeous little seventeen-year-old birds don't stay virgins for long, baby," she remembers that man, Maxwell Reed, remarking afterward. "Did you like it?" he asked. By her own admission, Joan hated it and found it "horrible, degrading, and demeaning." Small wonder that she felt this way. To her thinking, this first sexual encounter had been tantamount to rape.

On their first date, Reed had lured her to his apartment in a Georgian house. Naïvely, Joan thought they were going to one of London's trendy clubs; in the fifties these were frequently located in lofts and cellars of buildings. Though there were no etchings in evidence, the glossies of Reed alerted Joan to the fact that this was no club, but the actor's own lair, complete with a sofa bed covered with a zebra-skin rug and velvet cushions. He gave Joan her favorite cocktail, Scotch and Coca-Cola, but, unbeknownst to her, laced it with a bit of a Mickey Finn to get her in the mood for sex. She promptly fell fast asleep. Next thing, Joan woke to find herself entangled with Reed on his sofa bed and violently sick to her stomach. Through a haze of nausea, she recognized her black sweater and some of her undergarments ripped and lying on the floor. Only then did she realize that she was no longer a virgin. Somehow, with a brief stop home at dawn to shower and change and shed some tears, Joan managed to get to work on time the next morning.

No matter the circumstance, Joan was always vigilant about being punctual and prepared for her roles. Over and over again in interviews with people, whether producers, directors, or costume designers, who have spanned her whole career, the word "professional" would be among the first to spring to mind about her.

But it was her sexy look that led the late agent Bill Watts to sign her. He had seen her picture in the casting directory *Spotlight* while Joan was performing in repertory theater during her summer break from RADA. As Joan would demonstrate throughout her career, she would pay her dues here as well. With the Maidstone Repertory Company, she mostly served tea or helped backstage painting scenery. Though her father had arranged this stint for her, Joan did not try to pull rank, either. She only got to appear as the maid in the season's last play, Terence Rattigan's *French Without Tears*. Hollywood was, clearly, still some years away.

It had been her father's idea that she join a repertory company in order to get a listing as an actress in the casting directory. Joe Collins put the *Spotlight* ad in. This would be the last time that Joe Collins functioned, so to speak, as her agent. He believed, analogously, in that old adage about surgeons not operating on their own children. The directory listing, he figured, would attract an agent for her. It did just that. As Joan would put it, "He (her father) bought me a rep." But that did not mean that Joan would not seek his counsel in future years. Years later she would turn to her father for advice at the most crucial juncture of her career. His judgment call, delivered with passion and encouragement, would prove wholly correct.

But in the years prior to Joan's Hollywood entrance, the man in charge of her career was Bill Watts. Upon seeing Joan's picture in *Spotlight* with the Maidstone Repertory Company next to her name, he rang up immediately about a movie role in *Lady Godiva Rides Again*. She auditioned for the lead, as a beauty-queen winner, but got the part of a runner-up. But Joan was in good company. Jean Marsh, later known for her role as Rose in *Upstairs Downstairs* was another runner-up. Joan dropped out of RADA after a term to pursue roles on the silver screen. However, her affection and respect for the theater endures to this day.

Two weeks later Watts got Joan the part of a Greek maid in *The Woman's Angle*. But it would be her third role, in the low-budget thriller *Judgment Deferred*, that marked Joan for the first time as a "bad girl." The reaction, however, was anything but bad. As the once beautiful Lil, a convict's daughter who seeks pleasure in a town without pity, Joan got good press notices. Said the *Evening News:* "Although so young for her emotional role, Joan comes through with flying colors." But most importantly, Joan's performance caught the attention of two highly regarded partners in the movie business. They were producer Michael Relph and the late director Basil Dearden.

Michael Relph remembers his surprise at seeing Joan for the first time in an audition for *I Believe In You.* "Bill Watts specialized in having a stable of pretty girls," he explains. "So one rather knew what to expect from Bill Watts girls. But Joan had something extra." For starters, he recalls, Joan turned up "really dressed to kill" in a black satin suit, instead of the customary pair of old jeans. "She was a sensationally beautiful young girl," Relph says. "My partner was scared off. Joan was very self-possessed, and I think that was what made Basil (Dearden the director) hesitant. She was only sixteen or seventeen. She was almost too forthcoming. She had an amazing sophistication for a girl that age. We thought she was eighteen or nineteen. She was sharp and intelligent. We felt like we were taking a bit of a chance. But I felt she had star quality."

Joan landed the part of a streetwalker in the care of a probation officer. The play starred Celia Johnson. *I Believe In You* brought Joan good reviews once again. It also led indirectly to her disastrous marriage to Maxwell Reed. Through the male lead, Laurence Harvey, she met her future husband. In fact, she had used Harvey as her alibi date the night Reed got her drunk and raped her. In fact, she had pretended to her parents that she was going to a party with Harvey the night Reed got her drunk and raped her. Joan had figured that her parents would try to stop her from going on a date with Reed on account of his being so much older, thirty-one to her seventeen, and his reputation as a womanizer. Harvey, to their thinking, was still a young man, only in his twenties, and a gentleman.

The rape left Joan as much confused as horrified. Yet when Reed rang up the following afternoon to ask Joan to dinner, she accepted. Even to this day, the only explanation she can give is that as an insecure seventeen-year-old, with a problematic relationship with her own father, she needed to prove to herself that she was not unlovable— even in the face of such abuse. Reed apparently plugged into her psyche. "We started seeing each other, and he did not approach me sexually for some time," she remembers, "as though to atone for his fault." Once they resumed having sex, according to Joan, she gritted her teeth and tolerated it: "In fact I found it really boring, without a flicker of pleasure." Still, Joan could not let go of her fantasy of the handsome Reed, all six feet four and a half inches of him; the man who smoldered on the screen and had caused fireworks in her since she was a schoolgirl. A year later Joan married him.

Maxwell Reed was a British heartthrob of the fifties. He had a brooding nature that some women might mistake for sensitivity or mystery. Only, as Joan would discover, his brooding more often turned into bruising. Fourteen years older than Joan, he came from a rough Irish background, and before his acting career he had knocked about the world as a merchant seaman. He was recruited by the Rank Organization, England's most powerful and prolific movie makers in the fifties and sixties, while appearing in repertory in the North of England, and put in their youth company. Appropriately, the actor with wavy, black hair and dimples in his otherwise tough face, was billed by the stu-

dio as the "Beautiful Beast." His celebrity was
more a function of the glossy photos pumped out
by the Rank Organization than anything he did on
the screen. For the most part Reed was cast as a
boxer or underworld figure. By the time Joan left
him and moved on to Hollywood, his good looks
had begun to crumble along with his career.
Within a decade Maxwell Reed would be dead.

Joan, a brunette with sultry looks, was typed as a
wayward flashy girl, in contrast to the blond hero-
ines of the day. She proved to be more than sultry.
She smoldered. J. Arthur Rank, whose Methodist
beliefs frequently conflicted with his business in-
stincts, did not know how to handle the fireworks
that Joan apparently set off at his Pinewood Studios. So they put her out around other studios.
"Joan is alive," the *Sunday Express* said. "She has
bodily arrogance and vitality." Others referred to
her as "Coffee-bar Jezebel," the name used to describe teens who wore shirt blouses and skirts with
waists tightly pinched by cinch belts.

By now the British photographers hailed Joan as
"the most beautiful face in Britain." In turn, Joan
went out of her way to accommodate the press. No
interview was too much trouble. No matter how
weary she might be from work, she could find time
to pose for pinups. Self-serving as this attitude is
for a young actress, in Joan's case, it had as much
to do with her being an especially nice, polite person.

Reed also won his share of publicity. He got into
all the fan magazines read by girls like Joan and
Jackie. The day after Joan's eighteenth birthday
they got married at Caxton Hall in London. Years
later, Jackie would use Caxton Hall as the setting
for an aborted marriage between an air-head
centerfold model, Muffin, and a weeny-bopper
singing sensation, Little Marty Pearl, who has a

permanent case of arrested development. Though
the characters were certainly not based on Reed
and her sister Joan, ironically the title of the novel
was *The World Is Full of Divorced Women.*

There were moments, though, when art tended
to imitate life during Joan's first marriage. Between films, they did one theater gig of *The Seventh Veil* where Reed as a cruel piano teacher flings
Joan across the stage. The other, *Jassy,* featured
Joan as a young wife mesmerized and intimidated
by her vicious husband. Similar scenes were en-
acted during Joan's real-life honeymoon in
Cannes. Regrettably she was put in the role of a
battered wife.

Nothing in Joan's life had prepared her for this
role. Though her father was something of a bel-
lower, he had never so much as lifted a hand to his
wife or children. For the moment, though, Rank
rescued Joan from the abuse. They farmed her out
to Columbia Pictures for her first American film,
Decameron Nights. It was made in Madrid and Se-
govia, where Joan was only too happy to go, while
Reed stayed on in Cannes on their so-called honeymoon. Next she did *Cosh Boy,* called *Slasher* in the
United States. Playing the girlfriend of a mugger,
she gets pregnant and tries to commit suicide.

She worked next with Basil Dearden again.
Whereas Joan had been able to demonstrate promise as an actress in his earlier film, this time she
had to almost bury her talent. Reed was starring in
The Square Ring. Joan had a cameo role as a girlfriend, but found herself having to tiptoe around
her husband's enormous ego—not to mention phy-
sique—after he accused her of trying to upstage
him. Had Reed, in the midst of one of his jealous
rages, broken her nose, Joan might have landed
the lead role in her next film, *Turn the Key Softly.*
She lost out after refusing to get a nose job.

Filmed at a women's prison, it was the story of one day in the life of three women just let out of prison. Joan settled for the part of a young prostitute locked up for shoplifting.

By her next film Joan was again able to break away from her marriage for a brief spell. This time she went off on location in Majorca. As the spoiled brat Sadie in *Our Girl Friday (The Adventures of Sadie* in the U.S.), she goes on holiday with her parents, only to end up shipwrecked with three men on an island. This role resulted in the possibility of permanent exile from her husband. Twentieth Century-Fox was now thinking of bringing her to Hollywood. The timing could not have been more fortuitous. She would have good reason to want out of the marriage. Reed tried to persuade her to go to bed with a wealthy Arab sheikh for ten thousand pounds while he watched. "Never," Joan screamed. "I will never, ever do that. Never in a million years." And then, in her words, "I went home to Mummy."

Her mother, Elsa, accompanied Joan to Rome, the location for her next film, *Land of the Pharaohs*. It would be Joan's first big American film. Hollywood was now within her grasp and happily, she thought, out of Reed's reach. Joan played Princess Nellifer and wore a jewel in her navel. Soon Reed, his career waning, would turn up in search of real jewels, her engagement, wedding and topaz rings, and a $10,000 check. The demand came with threat that he would publish some nude pictures of Joan. After his death Joan, upon viewing them, realized they were really much ado about nothing. But during the moral fervor of the fifties, they might have done irreparable damage to her image. She capitulated to Reed's bribe. The movie's special-effects man acted as courier.

Whatever the cost, to Joan's thinking it was

worth it to be rid of Reed. Or so she thought. Ever the professional, Joan carried on as Princess Nellifer. Her "prince" would arrive in the form of co-star Sydney Chaplin, the second son of Charlie Chaplin. He was twenty-eight, and Joan was nineteen. The tall, dark, handsome Chaplin dazzled Joan with his wit, lifting her from the misery, despair, and mostly fear she had felt at the hands of her soon-to-be-ex husband.

An agent from the Famous Artists Agency negotiated the terms of Joan's seven-year exclusive contract with Twentieth Century-Fox. Joan stepped in and demanded more. It was a risk that even the agency's chief, whom Joan got involved in the dealings, worried might backfire. The risk paid off. Fox acceded to Joan's salary requirements. While Joan's father gave her high marks for her negotiating skills, he also questioned how capable his somewhat profligate daughter was at holding on to her money. "Jackie's sensible with money," their father noted in his autobiography. "Joan—I have a feeling—spends everything she earns." She started at $1,250 a week the first year, climbing to $5,000 in the seventh.

Once in Hollywood, Joan faced a formidable challenge, one that might have intimidated another neophyte actress. One of her first parts was that of lady-in-waiting to the legendary Bette Davis in *The Virgin Queen*. In the film Joan gets pregnant and is in love with Sir Walter Raleigh with whom Queen Elizabeth (Bette Davis) is also supposedly in love.

Her romance with Chaplin, who had moved to Hollywood to be with her, was also somewhat precarious. Missing Europe and failing to get work, he seemed to slip into periods of despondency. Joe Collins, who had met Chaplin back in England, observed how the young man bellyached about his father not doing enough to help him. In the meantime Joan paid the rent. It would not be the last time Joan paid her way. Throughout three of her marriages and all her relationships with men, she always bought all her own clothes, furs, most of her jewelry, and paid her own bills. With her fourth husband, Peter Holm, she also doled out an allowance and paid him a salary on commission.

At least Chaplin's friends had some intellectual and cultural currency. Among his and now Joan's social set were Gene Kelly, Adolph Green, Betty Comden, producer George Englund, and Paul Newman and Joanne Woodward, a couple more Connecticut than California. Sundays there was a regular volleyball game at the home of Kelly, who remains a friend of Joan. In her 1986 miniseries *Sins* she would cast Kelly, famed for his starring role in *Singing in the Rain,* as one of her made-for-TV husbands.

Yet those early days in Hollywood were, by her own account, a lonely time. "I was very shy," she told *Parade* magazine in 1985. "I still am; although I've conquered it to some extent. I think that probably has come from success and acceptance."

Always, she would return to London for succor. Hollywood, where she would move four times over three decades or so, could be harsh and indifferent. London was familiar. Even with its sunny clime, Hollywood could feel more chilly than rainy London town. Today there is a British slant to her friends who include fellow Brits Roger Moore, Michael Caine, Jacqueline Bisset, and, of course, sister Jackie. In recent years Joan has taken to jetting to London every few weekends to see her youngest daughter who is studying there. Before his recent death, she also visited her father. Sister Jackie, though more settled in her life here, intends to make London home once again in the future.

Almost from the moment Joan set foot in Hollywood, she got a lesson in how to preserve her English peaches-and-cream complexion. A friend took her over to the Beverly Hills Hotel, she relates in a 1980 video titled "The Making of Joan Collins," and pointed out people sunning themselves by the pool. "Their faces were shriveling in the sun," Joan remembers. "My friend said, 'Never go in the sun—it's a killer. Do you want to look like that at thirty or forty?' "

Though Joan likes to tan her body, she never exposes her face to the sun. She wears a hat and covers her face with sun block and makeup.

Though Joan advanced the cause of women her age by posing, at fifty, in *Playboy*, and today considers age "an attitude," it was something of a fixation in her early Hollywood days. "One of the things that stuck in my mind when first put under studio contract," she says, "is that at seventeen you had to do well and make money because by twenty-five you were washed out. Women, it was thought, started to lose their bloom then. I decided then on a particular regime. I was not going to fall apart at thirty."

Judging from her next part, Joan was still considered to be in full bloom. She played Evelyn Nesbit, a Gibson girl from the Floradora chorus, in *The Red Velvet Swing*. Marilyn Monroe, who would not have Joan's powers of survival, had turned down the role because she felt she was too old, at eighteen, to play a seventeen-year-old. The movie is about a fatal triangle. Joan, as Evelyn, is the wife of playboy Harry K. Thaw (Farley Granger) who shoots her lover, architect Stanford White (Ray Milland), dead in a jealous rage. Of all Joan's early films, according to her late father, that was Grandmother Hettie's favorite. He remembered Hettie reading him a press clipping in which Joan would admit that, "Men like to be kissed, and I like kiss-

ing them. If people don't like me, that's just too
bad!"

To which Hettie, Joan's biggest fan, responded:
"You see! She's learning to stand up for herself.
Speaking her mind. People will talk about her, take
notice of her." Then, pausing a moment, Joan's
grandmother frowned and inquired of no one in
particular, "I wonder just how much kissing she's
doing."

By then a would-be scandal was looming in
Joan's life. But it would have more to do with a
past mistake she thought she left behind in Europe
than her Hollywood behavior. A story in the *Los
Angeles Times* would report an announcement
from Maxwell Reed back in London that he was
suing her for $1,250, per month, on the grounds
that, in effect, he was a has-been while Joan was
pulling in big bucks. She now had a potential alimony drone on her hands. His legal action would
also prey on her reputation. Soon after, she was
tainted by the press as something of a free spirit. "I
was never the promiscuous hussy I was painted
as," Joan once said. "I always had a boyfriend. But
only *one* boyfriend at a time. But up until that time
in Hollywood, everything was very carefully
guarded. Many of the stars I know led extraordinary lives, in terms of promiscuity, drug addiction
and devilish, raffish behavior. But they were pro-
tected not only by the publicists, but also by the
columnists. And suddenly in the 50's, the studio
system started to slip, so the protection of the stars
slipped also. That's when I got the brunt of it, just
from being a real person and doing things like dating and partying that all normal young girls were
doing."

Her next boyfriend, Arthur Loew, Jr., won the
approval of Joan's father who was visiting her in
Hollywood at the time. Loew, Jr., grandson of the

founder of MGM and heir to the family's cinema and theater-chain empire, had just produced the Paul Newman film, *The Rack.* "I hope you're sensible this time," Joe Collins cautioned his daughter. "Don't treat sex as an aperitif." While Joan blushed, he advised further, "Now you've met someone nice; instead of wanting to run around all the time, it would do you good to stay in occasionally and watch television." To which Joan reportedly responded: "Daddy, what are you talking about? Watch television. I hate the horrid thing." To be sure, Joan would come to revise her thinking about this medium. Today, according to her late father, she has in her bedroom a television the size of a movie screen.

Joan's devotion to motion pictures would be reciprocated in kind. In 1956, after only about two years in Hollywood, Joan was voted the "Most Promising Star," "Face of the Year" and "Favorite Newcomer." It would never be the same for her the second—or even third—time around in Lotus Land. But never one to throw in the towel, Joan Collins would be back for a fourth and final round that would declare her the ultimate winner. She appeared that year in *The Opposite Sex,* based on Clare Booth Luce's *The Women.* She was a chorus girl trying to steal an older woman's (June Allyson) husband.

She acted the consummate bitch, rivaled only by Alexis in a later incarnation. But, per usual, Joan spewed venom on the screen rather than off it. Reed had her served with divorce papers on the set of this movie. Rather than engage in a prolonged and nasty battle, Joan conferred a quite generous lump sum, $4,250, on him. She had to empty their joint bank account in London and get an advance from Fox to cover it, as well as hefty legal fees. The whole episode added up to $10,000. The judge, who granted the divorce, seemed baffled by her generosity, in view of the short-lived marriage, with no children, and the fact that Reed, an able-bodied male in decent health, was certainly able to find some kind of work. But Joan was determined to buy her freedom from Maxwell Reed and any future harassment from him. Had Joan held out, refusing to pay out any money, the divorce would have dragged on and yielded messy headlines. Back in the fifties, long before California's community property law which provided for a no-fault dissolution of marriage, the main ground for divorce was adultery. Because of the scandal surrounding such divorce proceedings—accusations against corespondents, grainy pictures taken with telephoto lenses, and private eyes trailing errant spouses—it was better for both parties, especially public figures, to settle before the divorce became a declaration of war.

Joan got high marks, though, for behavior from the movie's director who told her father, visiting the set earlier on, "Mr. Collins, I'm pleased to say your daughter is very satisfactory; a strict time-keeper, very cooperative, very reliable . . . Temperamental actresses can be ruinous." Joan apparently tolerated the blisters from the washing powder used to create bubbles in a bathtub scene.

She was also getting raves from some of the leading men in her films. During the making of *Seawife* in the Caribbean island of Jamaica, Richard Burton, according to Joan, made an approach. Faithful to her role as a nun, shipwrecked on a desert island, albeit with Burton, she demurred. He was married at the time to his first wife. Joan, as the film crew joked, was "laying Loew," as it were.

It was also not her custom to become involved with producers or directors to get parts. On her next film, *Island in the Sun,* also made on location in Jamaica, Joan had to ward off the advances of producer Darryl Zanuck in a hotel corridor. In her private life Joan was very much a one-man woman. One man she was hard-pressed to resist was the King of Calypso, as Harry Belafonte was known then, and who was the star of this movie about racial tensions in the West Indies.

Back in the fifties, an affair with a black man was just too hot to handle. It could kill a career. Even in her autobiography, Joan never comes right out and says directly whether or not she and Belafonte ultimately had an affair. She would meet up with him later at the Coconut Grove in Los Angeles, where he was playing to overflow crowds and glowing reviews. Even as late as 1978, when *Past Imperfect* was originally published in England, there was little mention of Belafonte. In the updated American version six years later, in 1984, she provided few further details.

Whatever the case, Joan has always been very much the one-man woman then and now. Yet the temptress moniker would stick. That would amaze, among others, her own father. "Joan's relationships with men," he once said, "have often left me astonished at her naïveté. She has never manipulated any man, nor played one off against the other . . . Alexis would despise Joan as a stupid little ninny."

Before doing *Island in the Sun* and while *Seawife* was still in postproduction, Joan went home to Harley House for a while. She slipped easily back into the role of daughter, delighting in her mother's attention. Elsa Collins would scramble eggs for Joan, and they would chat and gossip together. Joan slept in her old bedroom. Jackie, now in Joan's Hollywood apartment, had appropriated it. But Elsa moved some of Joan's things back in.

Jackie had not been having an easy time of it

back home in London. It seemed that in her private life Jackie was acting out the early "bad girl" roles of Joan. "I guess I was really a juvenile delinquent," she admits. "I would pad my bed at night with pillows and be out the window. My parents were constantly threatening juvenile hall. Joan wasn't like me at all. She just went off and became a star." After getting expelled from Francis Holland at fifteen for smoking in the halls, her parents tried to dissuade her from a writing or journalism career. In fact, Jackie says she was brainwashed by them into thinking she did not have the qualifications to realize her dream of becoming an author. Her father suggested acting instead, and in an almost backhanded compliment, encouraged, "You're not bad looking. You can go to Hollywood and be a movie star like your sister." With hindsight, the late Joe Collins admitted this may have been a mistake. "It never crossed my mind, nor Elsa's, that Jackie might spend frustrating years in a profession where she was always in Joan's shadow."

Nonetheless, the suggestion did not trigger any resentment in Jackie, then. "It seemed like a pretty good idea at the time, so I went," she remembers. "Joan met me at the airport and gave me the keys to her car, the keys to her home, and told me to learn to drive."

For much of the year Jackie spent in Hollywood, Joan was frequently away on location elsewhere. While making a film in London, in fact, Joan occupied Jackie's bedroom in their parents' home for a few weeks. "I was virtually alone in Hollywood for a whole year," Jackie remembers fondly. "I was almost sixteen. It was one of the best years of my life." Though Jackie got a place in Twentieth Century's star-grooming school, she was unable to obtain a work permit. As a result she stayed only eleven months but managed to cram a lot of fun into that time. While in Hollywood, she reportedly had a schoolgirl fling with Marlon Brando. She has fond memories of him even to this day. "I first met him when I was a fifteen-year-old fan and he has continued to intrigue me," Jackie says. "To me he is the most talented actor of the twentieth century, not to mention at one time, the most attractive."

Joan had been only glad to arrange her painfully shy sister's first meeting with Brando, who later on functioned as a cover date for Joan during her love affair with his married buddy, producer George Englund. Whenever Joan was in town, she also took her baby sister to parties. "Having a sister who was a movie star was sensational," Jackie says. "To have entrée to meeting more or less anybody because she knew—and still does—everyone."

Jackie also had a close friendship with Shane Rimmer, a talented and respected character actor at least ten years older than she. Among his more recent roles, he played U.S. Secretary of State George P. Shultz in a TV drama *Breakthrough at Reykjavik* and Isak Dinesen's foreman in the film *Out of Africa*.

Jackie also met a whole host of ambitious actors and actresses, not all of them as high-minded as Brando or Rimmer and some of whom she now remembers as "chancers" and "just plain bums." She returned to London after eleven months in Hollywood. Even then Jackie the writer had a discerning eye. And she had retentive powers as well. The decrepit apartment complex, in which she placed her fictional character, the stud Buddy, in *Hollywood Wives* would be modeled on the apartment she shared in those days with Joan.

By then Joan was cooling off on Loew after almost fifteen months with him. Now she was busy with *The Wayward Bus,* a film adapted from the John Steinbeck novel, in which Joan played a nagging alcoholic wife who ran a diner for bus pit stops. She was duly sluttish in this role. But Jayne Mansfield, a costar, managed to retain her title as the "American Workingman's Number One Turn-on." Though the film bombed, Joan emerged with decent reviews. In part, it was because she had bags and circles drawn under her eyes to create a bloated alcoholic face.

Joan would reflect later on the irony of how beauty got her to Hollywood in the first place, but then prevented her being taken seriously. Yet she was determined to play beautiful women if the part was right. Around that time it was as if the spirit of glamorous Alexis was already incubating inside her. At a New Year's Eve party she and Loew finally broke up. The following exchange transpired on the dance floor: "You are a fucking bore," Arthur told Joan who zinged him back, "And you are a boring fuck."

Next she took a month-long holiday, her first in a long while, in Acapulco. There she met playboy Nicky Hilton, son of hotel tycoon Conrad Hilton and first ex-husband of Elizabeth Taylor. Back in Hollywood, Hilton would divide his attentions between her and actress Natalie Wood. It would be Joan calling it quits with Hilton in whom she saw the dark side of enormous inherited wealth. "Rich men's sons have a hard road to hoe," she once reflected. "It is almost the equivalent of being a beautiful girl." Ultimately Hilton would die from a drug overdose. "I've never been the sort of woman," Joan told *US* in 1985, "who was going to hitch her wagon to a shining millionaire." She adds emphatically: "I don't like people who take money from other people. I think it's abhorrent. I think that people who can't make it on their own and feel they have to suck money from a man are pathetic."

She was determined to make it all on her own. With her work schedule, however—some twenty films in various countries packed into six short years—it was a wonder that there was any time left for romance. No sooner had Joan returned from her Acapulco holiday than she was wanted almost immediately in Hong Kong to make *Stopover Tokyo*. The best to be said of that overacted film, according to Joan, was meeting its star Robert Wagner, who to this day remains a solid friend. In fact, in a recent magazine piece, "My Idea of a Sexy Man," featuring several actresses, Joan was quoted as saying, "Robert Wagner is the epitome of the sexy man. In addition to being utterly charming, he is handsome, elegant, always beautifully dressed and has manners to match."

Next she was off to Mexico for *The Bravados*, starring another Hollywood gentleman, Gregory Peck, who helped Joan get over her fear of horseback riding since riding was required for her role. Never a great animal lover, Joan is even a bit tentative around dogs.

Around that time, Joan felt as if she were riding off into the sunset. Or so she thought. The new man in her life was producer George Englund, a striking-looking man who had every quality she desired in a husband. Intelligent, witty, articulate, and romantic, Englund was, nonetheless, distinctly unavailable as a spouse.

Trouble was, Englund already had a wife, actress Cloris Leachman, as well as three sons with her. Though only about ten years older than Joan, Englund so impressed her with his witty and esoteric conversation that she regarded him as her Svengali. Had Joan not been so mesmerized, of course, she might have saved herself from what she would later describe as "twenty months of total agony."

Englund and Joan had met at Gene Kelly's house when she was dating Chaplin who, along with Loew, was a good friend of Englund. Joan also knew George's wife, Cloris, during those early days in Hollywood. But it was not until a promotion tour for *Stopover Tokyo* in New York that she and Englund spent time alone, at first for a romantic whirl around the Big Apple over a weekend and, after that, most weekday afternoons in Hollywood. If they went out evenings, Englund's good buddy, Marlon Brando, would be along as her alibi date. More alibis would follow. As a measure of Joan's naïveté, she believed Englund's story about separate bedrooms for him and his wife. Though Englund eventually did separate from Cloris, by that time there was too much water under the bridge for Joan and him to have a chance.

It would take a psychiatrist, an astrologer, a fling with a dictator's son under the stars in Palm Beach, and an incorrigible bachelor to wean Joan off George. The shrink, whom Joan saw thrice-weekly, had come recommended by Loew in the midst of Joan's 1956 divorce from Maxwell Reed.

"A girl with a father complex," Joan apparently learned from her shrink, "looking for affirmation of her desirability by enticing hard-to-get males." No amount of therapy, however, could talk Joan out of her obsession.

On a steamy summer night in 1958, at around eleven o'clock, Joan decided to drum up some drama of her own instead of watching what she considered to be the humdrum evening news. In an almost teenage frenzy, she drove by Englund's house to check out the separate-bedroom theory. Through a window she could make out the figures of both George and Cloris preparing to go to sleep.

Joan, suddenly realizing she had been duped, would be kept awake all night by rage in her solitary bedroom.

Around this time, Joan also consulted an astrologer who would accurately predict her nomadic life and her resilience in dealing with it. In the romance department, however, his reading may have done more to confuse Gemini Joan than rescue her. A Gemini, he pointed out, does not mate well with a Cancer, namely Englund; but Aries, among other signs, would be quite compatible. Trouble was, both her ex-beau Chaplin and future ex-fiancé, were Aries; in fact, they shared the same birth date. In her autobiography years later, Joan would remark, tongue-in-cheek, on the Aries factor: "Hitler and Reed were Aries, too."

No one could have predicted the brouhaha resulting from a tryst with Rafael Trujillo, Jr., son of the then-dictator of the Dominican Republic, on a yacht in Palm Beach. It was another desperate attempt on Joan's part to forget Englund.

Her so-called adviser in this matter was the worldly Zsa Zsa Gabor, who arranged Joan's date with Trujillo. The much-married Gabor told Joan that Englund was, in effect, a waste of time because he belonged to someone else. Fortunately, Joan did not fall head over heels in love with Trujillo. As she discovered, ex-post facto, he was also married and the father of six children. That information surfaced in newspaper headlines about the trinkets he lavished on several well-known film actresses. Among Trujillo's trinkets: a $10,000 diamond necklace to one Joan Collins.

Notwithstanding her own personal dramas, Joan managed to make some more films. One of them was *Rally 'Round the Flag, Boys!* with Paul Newman and Joanne Woodward, friends of Englund. Joan's circle of friends was quite an incestuous bunch. Newman helped her get the role as the witty vamp, Angela, married to a boring business-man in a small town.

In the film she tries to seduce Newman away from Woodward. In real life this could not have been further from the truth. Joan remains friends with them. During Joan's second marriage, she would live in their New York City apartment at one point for a month. And Joanne Woodward would be emotionally supportive of Joan during her first pregnancy. They even shared the same obstetri-cian.

Soon after starting work on *Seven Thieves,* in 1959, along came Warren Beatty; at only twenty-two, he was known more in those days as Warren-What's-His-Name and Shirley MacLaine's brother. Only by committing to Beatty was Joan able finally to wrench herself away from Englund. But George's marital status was ultimately matched by Warren's title as an incorrigible bachelor-cum-womanizer. Joan first glimpsed him in a Beverly Hills restaurant. They met up at a party where Warren impressed Joan from a distance with his piano playing. He bombarded her with phone calls with a passion that would also characterize his sex-ual appetite. As Joan noted in her autobiography, Warren could talk on the phone and make love at the same time. They moved in together. Sister Jackie told *People:* "Joan had a suite at the Chateau Marmont—a great glamorous suite. And I said, 'Oh, this is lovely, great.' She said, 'Yes, you won't actually be sleeping here. There is a little room at the top of the hotel where you will be sleeping.' I found at night Warren would change places with me." Jackie slept in his little attic room.

This romance was proving to be more memora-ble than the next few forgettable films she would make. There was trouble with Fox for turning down too many scripts in the last year, and now Joan was on suspension. In an unhappy yet somewhat amusing coincidence, around the time she was in *Seven Thieves* as a stripper, Joan was named one of "The Ten Worst Dressed Women" by gossip columnist Louella Parsons.

During her two years with Beatty, from 1959 to 1961, Joan got pregnant, had an abortion, and was engaged to him; in addition, her career began to fade while his was starting to bloom. At his insistence she turned down some roles to be with him. Or he would demean the scripts enough to dampen her interest. One film Joan rejected was *Sons and Lovers*. It was to be filmed in England. Warren wanted her to accompany him to New York while he prepared for his role in *Splendor in the Grass*. The actress who got Joan's part ended up with an Oscar nomination for it. Joan did the pseudo-Biblical bomb *Esther and the King* for a few brief weeks in Rome. It did nothing for her reputation, either, as a cooperative actress. The film's director was irritated when Joan wanted permission to fly to New York to assuage Warren's insecurities. She went. The weekend was spent arguing.

This would not be the first or last time Joan's heart ruled her head. But, ultimately, neither romance nor marriage would stop her from succeeding. Since arriving in Hollywood in 1954, she had nearly a dozen American films, albeit most of them mediocrities, to her credit. Now it was 1961. Incredibly, Joan was not yet twenty-eight.

Personal Sorrows

Back in England, in 1958, Jackie pursued some acting jobs. But she still wanted, above all, to become a writer. For her acting was more a matter of a livelihood than any special devotion to the craft. In London there were no barriers like the work permit denied her in Hollywood. Her problem now was not about getting parts, but instead shedding the irksome role of Joan Collins's little sister. She was almost seventeen.

Twice during this period Jackie Collins declared that she would change her name to either Jackie Douglas or Lee Curtis. Probably the latter surname was inspired by one of her favorite childhood stars, Tony Curtis; she had even kept his pinup picture on her wall. Realizing quickly, however, that this would not remedy her problem, she decided to stick with her own name. After all, she figured, she would then be known as "Joan Collins's Sister-Who-Changed-Her-Name." She also resented how reporters, assigned to stories on Joan, would try to make do by interviewing her.

The baby sister of Joan Collins vowed then and there to make *herself* a good story. Already she was spending endless hours writing in the privacy of her bedroom. She found herself absorbed by this activity and often writing into the wee hours of the morning. Her main companion was music, mostly modern jazz and rhythm and blues, playing on her Victrola in the background.

A former boyfriend, Tony Hall, remembers Jackie talking a lot about her ambitions in this area. "She always wanted to be a writer," he says. "She wanted to write children's television and books. She had a great affection for children. There was both an innocence as well as a naïveté about Jackie—I think she must be a Libra."

Hall met Jackie in 1958, just after she returned from Hollywood. Ten years her senior, he was twenty-six, and she sixteen going on seventeen. At the time Jackie was appearing in the movie *Rock You Sinners,* while he was moonlighting as a deejay in the Flamingo jazz club, owned by the producer of her movie. Of their first date, he remembers, "I went over to the studio to pick her up. She was in this dreadful British rock-and-roll film. We went to dinner. And things just started from there."

Over the next two and a half years they saw each other most every single day. Together they would go to movies, restaurants, jazz clubs, and dance clubs. "She was a wild, uninhibited jiver," he says of Jackie, who today prefers to sit out dances to look and listen in the clubs. She dressed in jeans and sweaters, but as for her makeup in those days, he says, "She wore either too much or too little." One of his fondest memories is of her teaching him to drive: "I bought this old car from a dealer in South London. Jackie would come along with her kid brother Bill and teach me to drive it. She was remarkably tolerant, very patient."

The couple shared a passion for music. "She turned me on to rather jazzy California music," he remembers. "One was Carl Jader the vibraphone player. She also brought back albums of Chet Baker singing. I had only known him as a trumpet player." This meant a great deal to Hall. "During the day I had a quite respectable job at Decca Records," he says, "but jazz was my motivating force then." Hall, in fact, had started his career by producing modern jazz albums and representing Blue Note in Britain before joining Decca as a label manager. During his thirteen-year stay there he also managed Atlantic with its all-star soul lineup, including Otis Redding and Wilson Pickett.

Jackie also preferred her after-hours work as a writer above acting jobs. As she explains, "I saw myself as an out-of-work writer who was acting to make money. I was still writing." Along with what Tony billed as "that dreadful British rock-and-roll movie," there were more forgettable roles. One was as April Quest in the television show *The Saint* with her pal Roger Moore. She had hoped to play a journalist in the BBC's first successful soap opera, *Compact*, about a woman's magazine, but ended up with the part of the star actress. Just like Joan, who initially played "bad girls," Jackie made her screen debut as a juvenile delinquent in *The Payoff*. Like Joan, she also did some repertory theater and even the same play, *French Without Tears*, earning her the billing "Lovely young sister of Joan Collins."

Of her acting career, which also included a two-week stint as a presenter of "Carroll Lewis and His Discoveries," a talent show promoted by her father, Jackie says, "If you blinked, you missed me." In retrospect, she believes that the acting jobs, as well as her Hollywood visits with Joan, were seminal to her writings. "Acting wasn't something I enjoyed or wanted to do. It was, in fact, something of an embarrassment to me. But it gave me insight into every angle of Hollywood and the movies." Though hardly attracted to a movie career, Jackie was already smitten with Hollywood after her year there. "I think California was always her dream since that trip," Hall recalls. "She loved the life there."

The Collins apartment at Harley House, Tony remembers, was always filled with agents and comedians and Lew Grade, once Joe's partner, playing cards when he went to collect Jackie for an evening out. "Her father was always one of the most likable—though certainly tough—theatrical agents in the business." He felt a special affection for Jackie's mother. "Elsa was such a warm and loving person. She was a super mother, lovely and kind to everyone. Jackie was more like her than Joan. She was far more inhibited than Joan who, like her father, could be volatile. Jackie was less self-confident, one of her most likable qualities. I think both girls were pretty scared of their father. I think he was closer to Joan, and I sensed that Jackie felt neglected."

Though Jackie, according to him, really liked her sister Joan, she adored her brother Bill. Every weekday evening after work Bill would accompany Jackie and Tony on their strolls in nearby Regent's Park. Hall remembers meeting Jackie and Bill on a holiday in the South of France. One incident showing Jackie's protective nature stands out in his mind from that trip: "We were in a pedalo (boat) with her brother Bill and there were some very strong waves near a rock in the water. Bill and I were scared, but Jackie took charge. She said she was a very strong swimmer and there was no problem. She about saved our lives." Of Jackie's relationship with Joan, he comments: "Obviously she lived in Joan's shadow. She did not speak about it much, but I think it was always there, always hanging over her. I think deep down Jackie felt Joan was better looking. I think she sometimes felt left out. Jackie always wanted to make it as a writer."

Though Hall says that he does not read the type of books she writes, he is, nonetheless, delighted about her enormous success. However, he does watch Jackie on talk shows. "I find it very strange to see the image Jackie Collins has today," her former boyfriend says, adding wistfully, "I think she's really the same person inside. Her soul hasn't changed. I think she's very quick and confident on television. Whether this is natural I don't know. Maybe through success it is genuine."

About the girl he knew then Tony rhapsodizes, "I found her very attractive, but I also found her to be a very, very nice girl. Jackie was extremely loyal to me. In fact, looking back on it, she was one of the nicest people that I ever went out with." Many people, including Joe Collins, thought the two would marry. Jackie's father even mentions this in his autobiography, *A Touch of Collins*. That did not happen. Quite to the contrary, their relationship ended on a very sour note—something Tony Hall says he regrets to this day. "Basically the relationship was going nowhere because I don't think either of us was really ready to get married. Her career was really unfulfilled then, and I had too much to do and couldn't be settled down. We were both much too immature. In the end I felt that somebody had to make a move to end it."

Hall would be the one to make that move. Ironically, he would do the thing that Jackie herself least liked doing in her own life at that time. Tony Hall became an actor for one brief moment. He played the part of a drunk. "I foolishly pretended to be drunk. I think really I should have become an actor because I played the part pretty convincingly. I came across as a pretty nasty piece of work trying to put her off. A nasty drunk. I believe she walked home from the jazz club. I can remember feeling terrible afterward, but feeling, well, maybe it worked. The sad thing is that I don't think she ever knew the real reason."

Since then, Hall, lean and fit, with an almost

boyish face despite the white hair framing it, has become quite a success in his own field. His loftlike office in Carnaby Street—the center of mod fashions in the sixties, now resembling an Arab bazaar —is headquarters to his Brampton Music publishing catalog, boasting several British chart hits, as well as his Manna Management Company. Under the latter umbrella, he has realized what he calls the fulfillment of a lifetime ambition: Britain's first all-black band, Loose Ends, topping the U.S. Black Charts in *Billboard* magazine. He is probably the only British manager today signing artists directly to America. Over the years in the business, with Tony Hall Enterprises, Britain's first-ever independent production company, he discovered and found record deals for major acts like Joe Cocker and Black Sabbath, and also handled the career of a black crossover arranger who worked on classic recordings by, among others, Elton John and David Bowie.

Tony Hall also knows the club scene, including London's Tramp, which is the only place he goes anymore, usually with his wife. Tramp, owned by Jackie's second husband Oscar Lerman, is where she observed some of the action as part of the research for her recent best-seller *Rock Star.*

Valuable fount of information though he may be, Tony Hall would not be one of those Jackie consulted for the book. In fact, Jackie has never spoken to Tony since the night he pulled off his drunk act. Though remaining on cordial terms with Joan and Bill—who was once a deejay at Tramp—and their father until his recent death, Hall cannot crack Jackie's sphinxlike reaction to him. "Even if we were all sitting at the same table at Tramp," Hall claims, "Jackie would not speak to or even acknowledge my presence. I get along fine with her husband, Oscar. And Johnny Gold, his partner, is a good friend. I'm sad because I really did like Jackie a lot. I think she was a smashing person and still do. She wasn't at all what the world reading her books may think she is. She was naive and had high moral standards. Just a thoroughly nice girl. I really enjoyed the time I spent with her." Then, like the deejay that he was in bygone days, Hall says that he would like to send a message out to her. "I'd like," Hall says softly, "to say I'm sorry to her."

Much like some of her strong female characters, triumphing over humiliation, Jackie did not lose all that much sleep, it seems, over Tony. Within a few months she got married to her next boyfriend, Wallace Austin, from a wealthy London Jewish family in the clothing business. "I was very surprised," admits Hall, "when she married him. I met Wally once."

They married in December 1960. Jackie was nineteen, and Wallace twenty-six. Educated in America, he was now a successful dress manufacturer. They had met at a party. According to the late Joe Collins, the courtship was formal and correct: "Wallace gave Jackie a huge diamond engagement ring." As Jackie remembers, "I think I married him because everybody said I couldn't—that he wouldn't want to marry me."

Jackie's father, though, got quite a shock when he discovered the Austins were planning a wedding reception for some 600 people at London's Grosvenor House on Park Lane, exclusive and pricey as, say, a similar affair at New York's Plaza or Pierre Hotel. "We must hire a ballroom at one of the best hotels," Joe Collins remembers Austin's mother insisting. "I think Grosvenor House." Joe's first reaction was a gulp. Probably it was one of the rare times in his life that he would be caught off guard. Then, said he, "That's a very big ballroom." The matter was ultimately resolved: Jackie's father would foot one third of the bill and hire the band. The Austins absorbed the bulk of the cost. The wedding went off without a hitch. Joe Collins was glad to give his daughter a day to remember. Indeed, Jackie looked beautiful in a white satin bridal gown which cost about $800. It seemed that almost everyone was invited from both the Collins and Austin sides of the family, to celebrate.

Joan flew in from Hollywood with her fiancé Warren Beatty, who was now making his second big film, *The Roman Spring of Mrs. Stone*, in London. By now, Beatty had gotten considerable attention costarring with Natalie Wood, before then a child star, in *Splendor in the Grass*. Despite his promising career, Warren did not strike Joan's father as much of a certainty in the marriage department. Though Joe Collins thought Beatty was obviously attractive and well-mannered, he also sensed something else. "There was a restlessness about Beatty that told me he was not yet ready to settle down."

Jackie must have also figured then that Warren would not become her brother-in-law. "Like everyone else," she told *People* many years later, in 1985, "I got propositioned by Warren. But since I turned his proposition down, Joan and I never shared a boyfriend. The possibility was there, let's put it that way. But Warren would proposition a chair if it looked at him sideways."

It was becoming clear to Joan, as well, that her relationship with Beatty was heading nowhere. While Jackie went off on her honeymoon to Mexico, Joan moved back into Harley House. She was glad to do this because her mother, Elsa, after a successful operation to remove a malignancy, was still a bit weak and in need of some help around the house.

Once back from her honeymoon, Jackie settled

into a new house in the tony Hampstead Heath in North London, about twenty minutes by car from the West End and not unlike New York's Scarsdale or Cleveland's Shaker Heights. Hampstead was also famous for, among other things, the home of Anna Freud (the only daughter of Sigmund) and her clinic for children. One of Anna Freud's works, *War and Children*, was about the effect of the Blitz on children who, like Jackie and Joan, had lived through it, but most of whom had been yanked from the comforting presence of a mother and put in shelters. At least Jackie and Joan had had their mother to comfort them in that period. Today, Hampstead is populated by largely upper-middle-class professionals, as well as a smattering of artists and oddball characters, among them Boy George, who lives in a neo-Gothic house that looks like something out of the Addams family.

Joan had forebodings about Jackie's marriage. In fact, she had tried, apparently to no avail, to talk her out of it. She worried that by marrying so young, Jackie might be making the same mistake that she had earlier with Maxwell Reed. Within a year of her marriage, Jackie gave birth to a baby girl whom she and Wallace named Tracy. The birth of Jackie's first child would turn out, however, to be something of a godsend. Tracy, as the first grandchild, would breathe hope and joy into Elsa's now-waning life.

During the last days Joan spent with Elsa she would gain a whole new understanding of her mother. Much as Joan loved her deeply and irrevocably, she was full of ambivalence about some of her mother's puritanical teachings. "Men are no good," her mother repeatedly instilled in Joan as a child. "They only want one thing." Just as soon as Joan became aware of the male sex, by her own admission, she deliberately set out to debunk these myths. In the case of her first husband, Maxwell Reed, clearly, Joan's rebellion backfired on herself. The blame she fixed, in part, on her mother would be sorted out on an analyst's couch. But, with time, she would also come to hold on to some of her mother's advice in this area.

In those precious days with her mother, Joan was also able, more importantly, to liberate herself from the rage that she had felt at the way Elsa had tolerated Joe's domination of her life. Jackie, with a husband and child of her own, was not as obsessed as Joan, then, with their parents' relationship. She had her own family, a buffer of sorts against the pain Joan felt then over her mother's life. Now Joan could almost look on her parents' marriage with a certain forgiving attitude that came with understanding and which also produced a certain peace inside herself.

In her autobiography, Joan would detail the way her father had taken over her mother's life. Among other things, whatever he said was the law in the Collins household. She quoted her father thus: "I pay the bills around here," he would roar if anyone dared remonstrate or argue with him. "If you're so clever, you make the money to support us all. Then I'll listen to you." He used money like a rod to beat his wife and children into submission. Further, according to Joan, he took over her mother's identity. Even the friends she had before her marriage were traded in for her husband's cronies. And he reduced her, in Joan's words, to "a dumb blonde role," causing her to doubt her own intellectual capacities and to adopt his opinions. "He, being a male chauvinist," she observed, "before we even knew the meaning of the phrase, ruled the roost totally."

But as her mother lay dying, Joan came to understand that this circumstance was more a

generational problem than Elsa's own personal af-
fliction. Of course, for someone as bright and per-
ceptive as Joan, she must have known this fact all
along. But accepting it emotionally was another
thing altogether. Nor would Joan, as an adult presumably in charge of her own life, be obliged to
copy this way of life. Ironically, she had done just
this, first with Reed and then with boyfriends
whom she tried to please by submerging her own
needs in their lives.

It was as if Joan had an epiphany about her
mother's life in those last days: she realized Elsa
Collins *adored* her husband. Whether or not she
knew any differently, which, clearly, women of her
generation did not, her mother had chosen the life
she wanted and was, in her own fashion, satisfied
with it. "I never understood," Joan said to herself
repeatedly, "how she could be so loving to someone who treated her so badly." Joe Collins would
describe his wife as "peace-loving." Now a great
peace would wash over Joan who remembers her
mother's "sparkling blue eyes and high cheekbones
and joie de vivre." With her husband and all her
children—and grandchild Tracy—around to comfort her, Elsa Collins died knowing her family had
truly loved her.

Elsa Collins died on May 8, 1962, at only fifty-six.
Though she had not lived long enough to witness
her daughters' triumphs, at least she had experi-
enced the pleasure of holding her grandchild, just
as she had her own children, and had touched all
their lives in a deep and abiding way. Joan was
only twenty-nine, Jackie twenty-one, and Bill sixteen, when they lost their mother. Each of them
would remember her in his or her own way. Her
name would be on the flyleaf of Jackie's first novel,
The World is Full of Married Men. The dedication in
the *Joan Collins Beauty Book* reads: "In memory of

my mother, Elsa, who guided me in the right direction." In Joan's autobiography, *Past Imperfect*, the dedication again honors her: ". . . And for my mother, Elsa. I wish she could be here to share it all with me."

All the children were near Elsa in her last days. Bill, only a teenager, was still at home. Jackie brought her mother the bundle of joy that was her newborn baby every day. Her marriage was a source of comfort to Elsa, who wished for Joan the same promise of a settled life with a husband and child. Elsa and particularly Joe, who was Jewish like the Austins, felt warmly toward their new son-in-law Wallace.

She would be laid to rest in Hampstead Cemetery not far from Jackie's house. Within two years of Elsa's death there would be another family tragedy. Wallace Austin would be found dead in a car in the county of Hampshire, north of London. Though he and Jackie were divorced by then, their child was now left fatherless, a heartache for Jackie. The marriage which had seemed at first to be so appropriate, if not perfect, had been doomed, in fact, from the start. "A tragic marriage," Jackie recalls. "He was really very sick. He was a manic depressive. A fabulous person. But he was put on drugs—methadrine—for the depression." Wallace Austin, she believes, overdosed on his medication.

Despite her own tragic losses, first her mother and then the father of her child, Jackie found enough strength inside herself to console her father. "A tower of strength" is the way Joe described her. She also helped her brother through this period. Always, she had shown a maternal instinct for him.

Though only in her early twenties herself and suffering her own immense grief, Jackie moved past her own sorrows to provide an emotional

cushion for others. She demonstrated her powers
of survival even then. Though saddened by the
death of her ex-husband, whom she would remember as "my Jewish prince," she accepted the fact
that, in her words, "You can live your life trying to
save someone for only so long."

Her main responsibility now was to raise her
young daughter Tracy and to begin a new chapter
in her life.

Jackie the Novelist

When Jackie Collins first met Oscar Lerman on a blind date at his now-defunct London club, Ad Lib, all he could talk about was his recent bout with jaundice. This apparently did not impress Jackie too much. What did engage Jackie, however, was his immense interest in her unfinished manuscripts. Later on in this book we will discover how Oscar has remained Jackie's most loyal fan and supporter. But for the moment Lerman, a Philadelphia-born businessman and owner of the trendy London nightclub called Tramp, remembers how taken he was with Jackie's written works. "I was shocked at how good they were," he says. Indeed, it was Oscar's encouragement that prompted Jackie to finish *The World Is Full of Married Men*, published in 1968. By then, the couple had married, in 1966, at sister Joan's home in Beverly Hills.

The book satisfied the revenge fantasies of betrayed wives. Its protagonist, David Cooper, a middle-age advertising executive, gets involved in a torrid affair with a young model. Though he ultimately realizes his mistake, by then it is too late because his ex-wife, Linda, has already met someone whose previous wives cheated on him and who will be faithful to her. As Linda sails off into the sunset with her new husband, David slips into a semialcoholic stupor that renders him virtually impotent and only able to perform with his mousey spinster secretary. Even the model ends up with a better deal. Jackie got the idea for the book at a party. "The world is full of married men," Jackie recalls a woman saying to her quite cheerfully. And there it was, the title, full sprung.

"It wasn't so hard to start," says Jackie Collins, who had always been on the sidelines observing, but this time she had someone, her second husband, encouraging her to finish. The book, she explains, was a different kind of novel than what was being written at the time. "If a married man can play around in marriage, a woman can, too," Jackie says. "The women who were writing at the time—Edna O'Brien, Penelope Mortimer—all had women going off to the country and having nervous breakdowns over married men. I was writing a woman who was not in literature at the time."

Without an agent, but with the strong support and encouragement of her husband, Jackie sent off the manuscript to a publisher. It was accepted. Within a week of its publication in England, *The World Is Full of Married Men* made the best-seller list. Jackie comments: "I wanted to get a dig at men in the book. It's all right for a married man to have affairs, but they're surprised to find out that their wives do, too!" When the book was banned in Australia, Jackie asked wryly, "What's the matter? Don't you have married men there?"

If an author is somebody who writes books that sell, clearly the success of her first book in both England and America gave Jackie Collins claim to this title. From then on, it was big advances and huge publicity campaigns for novelist Jackie Collins.

Many people raised their eyebrows at the steamy sex scenes in her first novel. But there was more to come—they hadn't seen anything yet. The novels *The Stud* and its sequel, *The Bitch*, were next. She chose a fashionable London discotheque as the setting for both. No doubt, her marriage to a club owner gave her better access and more intimate insight than most writers into London nightlife. It would not be the last time discos figured in scenes from her novels.

The main character in both books is Fontaine Khaled, a disco owner whose life-style exceeds her bank account. Married to a wealthy Arab businessman, who ultimately divorces her, she is a woman greedy in her desire for both men and money. Fontaine exploits men sexually and then dumps some of them right out on their derrières.

Some people faulted both books for being too sexually explicit. One of them was British romance novelist Barbara Cartland. "Filthy, disgusting, and unnecessary," she sniffed at *The Stud.* Jackie, meanwhile, was probably laughing all the way to the bank. She also earned the title "Britain's Answer to Harold Robbins and Jacqueline Susann." Though admiring of both writers as storytellers, she took issue with the comparison on another front: the war between the sexes.

Of both Robbins and Susann, she says: "Each, respectively, takes sexual sides. I'm right in there writing honestly about men and women and getting the balance right. I like to see good girls win in the end. What I actually am is a moralist." Jackie continues: "I love Harold Robbins' men. But my women are the aggressors. A lot of American writers have become gynecologists rather than storytellers. I believe in marriage, and my message to men is don't screw around with women because they can turn around and screw you back." At the same time, Jackie advises women, simply, "Keep the home fires burning."

Jacqueline Susann's biographer, Barbara Seaman, also sees other differences between the two

Jackies. "Jackie Susann's books were autobiographical and she thought that's what women's lives were really like," she says. "I don't get the feeling that Jackie Collins bases her novels on her own life." While both are what Seaman labels "brand-name authors," she draws still another distinction between the two. "Jackie Susann didn't understand the difference between herself and Nabokov and Philip Roth and why critics did not take her seriously. Jackie Collins is more clever." Seaman comments, "She's self-made, but calculated about it."

Just as the shock waves from her first three novels were dying down, Jackie socked it to the public again with more randy razzmatazz; namely *Sinners, The Love Killers, The World Is Full of Divorced Women, Lovers And Gamblers,* and *Chances.* But in contrast to the stir she was creating in the outside world, life on Jackie's home front was extremely settled and disciplined. Oscar and Jackie now had two children of their own, Tiffany and Rory, as well as Tracy, from her first marriage to Wallace Austin. The Lermans were comfortably installed in a four-bedroom home in London with marble tables, Art Nouveau statues, and 1920's porcelain miniatures.

Hardly the bored housewife, Jackie kept to a strict schedule. Rising at 7 A.M. to prepare the family breakfast, do the housework, and read the papers, she could finally sit down at her desk to write at around 9:15 A.M. Over the next nine hours she would fill the exercise books, in which she writes longhand, with around 5,000 words, her usual daily output. Often she would not even pause for lunch, and just have some black coffee.

When Jackie wanted to write a romantic passage, she would listen to black soul singer Isaac Hayes for inspiration. She found that his music created the atmosphere she was trying to convey at that moment. Not until 6:30 P.M. did Jackie put down her pen for the day.

Jackie was equally disciplined about her family life. Most nights were reserved for Oscar and the children. But two or three nights a week, the happily married couple would slip out for a few hours to Ad Lib. Here they would spend time among club regulars such as Michael Caine, Mick Jagger, Rod Stewart, and Ringo Starr. Unlike some writers, Jackie did not fuel herself with drinks. In fact, she has never been keen on alcohol. Her standard order: Perrier water. When she takes the occasional drink, it is usually something exotic or fruity like a banana daiquiri. "I have very unsophisticated tastes in booze," she reveals. "Things like milkshakes with a hidden kick." In fact, Jackie's main indulgences at the time were two American cars: a silver Ford Mustang and a black Cadillac Seville.

Soon after the publication of *Lovers and Gamblers* in 1977 Jackie and Oscar decided to move to California. As Jackie remembers, "I woke up one morning. My books were doing very nicely. In England they were number one. And I thought, I want America. And I just packed up with my kids and my dogs and went there. We lived in the Beverly Hills Hotel for three months, which is somewhat bizarre, but I got wonderful research." The biggest and best was yet to spill out of Jackie's pen.

The novel would take a broad look at Tinsel Town and earn her the sobriquet "Hollywood's Margaret Mead." It would be called *Hollywood Wives* and catapult Jackie Collins to international fame as a novelist. Reviews were mixed and many. *The New York Times* said: "The novel is crammed with beautiful people scheming to advance themselves. No detail of their designer clothes or Rolls Royces has been omitted." It went on: "But Miss Collins is at her raunchy best when describing the collisions between rivals at parties or in bedrooms. She also excels at pacing her narrative, which races forward, mirroring the frenetic lives, chronicled here with wit."

Gossip columnists around the world, meanwhile, busied themselves with trying to get the scoop on the true identities of her fictional characters. Hollywood wives themselves joined in the guessing game. In an article she penned for *TV Guide,* Jackie described the reaction thus: "If one more Hollywood wife slides up to me and says, *'Hollywood Wives* is the book I should have written,' I'll scream!" She twitted in the same piece: "When would she have written it? Between manicures? Body massages? Three-hour lunches? Or maybe she could have fitted it in between a shopping trip to Rodeo Drive and the organization of yet another perfect little party for 150 A-list guests!

"But then"—Jackie pointed out—"the easier you make things seem, the more people think they can do it, and everyone thinks she can write a book." Then, tongue-in-cheek, Jackie concluded, "Indeed —one day when she has time, she will do so!"

Well, Jackie has some news for everyone. "It is not so easy," she says. "It's hard, lonely work, and I mean work. To shut yourself away for months on end takes tenacity, determination, a strong masochistic streak, and a great belief in what you're doing." *Hollywood Wives,* Jackie says, was, nonetheless, a labor of love. "Creating fictional yet very true-to-life characters from the Hollywood mélange was a challenge," she explains. "For Hollywood is full of clichés and leaving them out would not be a truthful picture of Hollywood." Some people suggested that the novel read more like a roman à clef.

Even a year after publication, the hardcover and paperback editions remained on the best-seller lists in Britain, America, Australia, and Ireland. Its success proved a theory of this British-born author: "In America there is no need for a Royal Family because the great old movie stars such as Bob Hope, Katharine Hepburn, and the late Cary Grant are national monuments, and are treated with a certain reverence and respect. Let's face it—even Ronald Reagan was a film star. And if Paul Newman or Robert Redford made a serious stab at the Presidency, he'd have a very good chance."

The worldwide attention lavished on the book was matched only by the flap in her own backyard. Hollywood natives were, to say the least, nervous. "Everybody wanted to know who was in it and if they were portrayed in a flattering light," Jackie remembers. "Lines of chauffeurs and maids were dispatched to the bookstores to pick up a copy immediately. Bookstores in Beverly Hills sold out the first day."

Their jitters did not stop. Jackie's phone started ringing off the hook. Jackie remembers a typical call, which went something like this, " 'Jackie, darling, I have just read *Hollywood Wives* and it's such fun, a really accurate picture of Hollywood. And I don't recognize a soul!' Next came a pause and then, 'But, of course, Gina Germaine is (well-known sex symbol named) and Ross Conti has to be (fading macho superstar named) and everybody knows that Sadie La Sallie is (powerful female agent named).' " Dozens of phone calls later, Jackie had the last laugh: "They all knew exactly who everyone was supposed to be; only they named all different people." From Jackie's Hollywood friends came reactions ranging from "pure fantasy" to "right on the mark" to "too much sex" and "not enough sex." "Well," says Jackie, "you can't win 'em all!"

One remark that particularly amused Jackie

came from a Hollywood wife who inquired of the author: "If everyone in Hollywood was horizontal the entire time, then how did any work ever get done?" Another Hollywood wife collared Jackie at a party and accused her of writing about her husband. "He is Ross Conti," the wife reportedly insisted. "How did you find out all his secrets?" She was somewhat deflated, according to Jackie, by the answer. "You could trip over Ross Conti in Hollywood," the author said of the philandering character Conti. "There are plenty of them around."

Hollywood Wives seemed to be on the tip of everyone's tongue. "All of a sudden it became part of the language," Jackie reports. "Newspapers and magazines began making lists. Television gossip programs started thrusting microphones at potential victims as they arrived at parties and premieres. 'Are you a Hollywood wife?' they would demand to know." According to Jackie, some of the victims gave a "frosty no."

Hollywood Wives soon became a dirty word—"two dirty words," Jackie remembers. "Nobody would admit to being A Hollywood Wife." Despite the notoriety, it was never Jackie's intention to offend or wound. Nor did she mean to suggest that all the women in the area were marked as "Hollywood wives."

"I was certainly not condemning every woman in Hollywood who has ever bought a designer dress, had a manicure, or spent her day lunching, shopping, and trashing everyone in town. Heaven forbid!" she explains. "I wrote about a group of women who are inclined to think of nothing else but material possessions and their queenly position in Hollywood society. Wives of stars, producers, studio heads who truly believe they are loved and adored for themselves, not because of who their husbands are. What a nasty shock they get when their divorce comes!"

Jackie also had some kind words. "There are many terrific Hollywood wives—smart, sexy women who look beautiful and yet care about many good causes and devote themselves to charities," she defends. "They realize that in Hollywood you play the game and do not take yourself too seriously." And she states emphatically, "To be sure, there are some fantastic, long-lasting marriages."

Ever since her first visit to California while still in her teens, Jackie Collins has always felt a special affection for the place. Writing *Hollywood Wives,* by her own admission, satisfied part of her fascination with the area. She likes to observe all the people, "not just the rich and famous," she explains, "but also the kids who flock to Hollywood from all over America to find fame and fortune, and quite literally, their places in the sun."

Though some people regarded the novel as scandalous or, as she mimics, "all about sex and sin in big bad Hollywood," she has some more astonishing news. "I actually toned it down," she says. "It is based on truth. Most of the wilder goings-on—to protect the not-so-innocent Hollywood—have always generated more than their fair share of gossip and scandal. I merely mirrored what happens."

It is hardly surprising that one of the questions most frequently asked of her is how she researches her books. "Very, very carefully," she answers. "I get invited to a lot of parties, and the fun for me is to arrive, grab a ringside seat, sit back, and observe. People-watching is a fascinating occupation."

One party scene in *Hollywood Wives* lasts through several chapters. "It is very authentic," Jackie assures her public. "While attending Hollywood parties I go off to the bathroom and jot down actual dialogue—amusing, accurate, outrageous, and very, very Hollywood." She also watches the wives chatting among themselves. "The ladies come out with things that even I don't believe," she says with a chuckle. "They make a men's locker room seem tame."

The book grew out of a lunch at an exclusive Beverly Hills restaurant: "I can remember looking around at a sea of lifted, impeccably made-up faces. These women were groomed to the eyeballs in designer clothes and diamonds. Yet they had no individual style—they all looked the same. Ah, I thought, Hollywood wives, and the book was born."

Jackie admits to relying, in part, on a bevy of researchers, none of them salaried. "I have some great friends who call me up and tell me some great pieces of gossip," she says. "I really don't need to set foot outside my house—I'd still know everything that goes on. Hollywood can be wild even though the rich and famous deny it. But let's face it. Does a professional wrestler ever admit the bout is fixed?"

The success of *Hollywood Wives* was not the only pleasure Jackie Collins got from the book. She also had, by her own account, great fun with it. In fact, unbeknownst to the world, its twin, *Hollywood Husbands,* was already gestating in her mind. It would take a probing look at the men in Lotus Land. Meanwhile, *Hollywood Wives* was adapted for a miniseries by Aaron Spelling Productions, which billed it as "A revealing six-hour look at Hollywood's more colorful saints and sinners." *The Washington Post*'s critic had another opinion: "Yet another lewd-minded super trashy collaboration between ABC-TV and producer Aaron Spelling," he decried. "One can enjoy it providing one's brain is put on hold."

Yet it became a huge commercial success. Its ratings went through the roof. It also boasted a stellar cast that included Candice Bergen, Mary Crosby, Stephanie Powers, Angie Dickinson, Anthony Hopkins, and Rod Steiger. They seemed to share the audience's enthusiasm. Mary Crosby, who played Karen Lancaster, a self-assured, catty divorcée, said, "When I read the book, I couldn't wait to sink my teeth into it." Anthony Stevens, in the role of the stud, Buddy, did not rely only on the script. "Reading the book really filled in the character for me," he said. "It's not exactly *War and Peace*, but it's great trash," said Suzanne Somers, cast as a sexpot actress. "It was my first trampy lady. She is a rotten, conniving, manipulative, blackmailing woman." Angie Dickinson, playing a ruthless agent, summed it up: "It's the gossipy stuff we all love."

Between Hollywood wives and husbands Jackie would come up with still another winning title: *Lucky*. A sequel to *Chances*, it also became a bestseller. Her reported million-dollar advances were proving to be a shrewd investment on the part of her publishers. Again this book produced mixed reviews. "Miss Collins's latest and tenth book is like the others," said *The Wall Street Journal*. "Embarrassing to pick up and impossible to put down." The *Hollywood Reporter* enthused: *"Lucky* reads like the publishing equivalent of a firecracker." And the Washington *Times* proclaimed, "Jackie has done it again."

Lucky picked up where *Chances* left off with luscious Lucky Santangelo and her lusty old Daddy Gino, ex-mobster-turned-hotelier. *People* magazine, lashed out at *Lucky:* "Trying to read this book is like staring into a big cauldron that is bubbling over with every half-baked idea ever spewed out by Jacqueline Susann, Harold Robbins, and all the writers of television soap operas." The *People* reviewer continued: "It is a hard-core novel. Awful novel. A profusion of worn-out plots and characters revolve around the sexy daughter of an ex-mobster and now hotel owner in Las Vegas." And as if that wasn't enough, the magazine took another swipe: "Collins is to writing what her big sister is to acting."

Of *Lucky*, Collins had this to say: "She's a great fantasy character for me. If I had my life to live again I'd quite like to be like her. Because she lives her life with the freedom of a man." Lucky, she says, was named after the mobster Lucky Luciano. In response to criticism that some of the details were far-fetched, Jackie told *US* magazine, "I've been on the yacht I describe in *Lucky*. And they actually do sell $5,000 mink-lined bikinis in Las Vegas because I've hung around the MGM Grand Hotel there and seen it."

Neither her novels nor their sequels, Collins claims, are repeat performances. "I don't think I write to any particular formula," she told one interviewer. "I write about people who are living very glamourous lives, eventually. But I also write about people who don't have anything and want to get there. And, maybe, I write about the desire for success and power quite a lot, but the characters are different."

Hollywood Husbands, her next book, caused a stir just as the story of Tinsel Town's wives had done. "My hats off to Jackie Collins," said *The Washington Post*. "A sizzling novel about Tinsel Town's cheatingest males." But apparently there was still no placating *People*. Said its reviewer, "Reading Jackie Collins is like indulging in too much cheap champagne at a party. It's fun at first, but before long your head starts to ache and by the next day, it's hard to remember who was there and what anybody said." Observed one *New York Times* reviewer: "Jackie Collins's strong suit is writing about women." With still another blockbuster under her belt, Jackie Collins continued her reign as one of the world's best-selling and richest authors.

She did not rest on her laurels. For Jackie, it was back to work. The result of her labor: *Rock Star,* a punishing story of drugs and sex in the world of rock music, where hopes and dreams collide with ambition and avarice. Or, as British television personality Alan Whicker described it, "It's about a musical world where the women are all 39 D and the men throb with desire." Said England's *Sunday Mirror:* "Certainly Jackie's 12th novel maintains her sexy sizzler and racy read reputation."

Indeed, the book lives up to its billing. It opens with three characters, all singers, on their way to the most expensive charity function ever. They are Kris Phoenix, white, former Maida Vale window cleaner; Bobby Mondella, black, once a men's room attendant at a New York disco; and Rafealla, an exotic café au lait creature. The story, told, in part, in flashback, allowed Jackie to draw on her knowledge of the British scene. "Kris is my favorite character," she told the *Mirror,* "because he is the English one, and I'm able to use all the English expressions I usually have to quash—you know, stuff like 'Wanna get your leg over, mate.'"

Once again a guessing game ensued, and Jackie did nothing to stop it. "Everyone is going to say it's Rod Stewart or Mick Jagger or one of the Beatles," Jackie teased. "Or they're going to think Rafealla is Whitney Houston or Sade or somebody like that. As for Bobby, you could think maybe Teddy Prendergast or perhaps Luther Vandross with a sprinkling of Stevie Wonder." With sufficient interest

Joan and first husband Maxwell Reed on their wedding day in 1952.
(*AP/Wide World Photos*)

Joan and her then-husband-to-be Anthony Newley in 1962.
(*AP/Wide World Photos*)

Sisterly support: Jackie and Joan prior to the court hearing that would grant Joan her divorce from Maxwell Reed in 1956. (*AP/Wide World Photos*)

Jackie as a young bride on her wedding day in 1960. Despite her smile here the marriage would eventually end in tears.
(*AP/Wide World Photos*)

Hollywood Sisters Jackie and Joan together in London, 1977.
(*AP/Wide World Photos*)

The book that started the story: Authoress Jackie Collins and her first novel, *The World is Full of Married Men* (London, 1968).
(*AP/Wide World Photos*)

Joan Collins in a different role, as mother with children Sacha (left) and Tara at Leonardo da Vinci Airport, 1968.
(*AP/Wide World Photos*)

A happy family: the late Ron Kass and Joan enjoy the company of their daughter, who they nursed back to life with love following a car accident.
(*AP/Wide World Photos*)

Alexis in a different habit.
(*AP/Wide World Photos*)

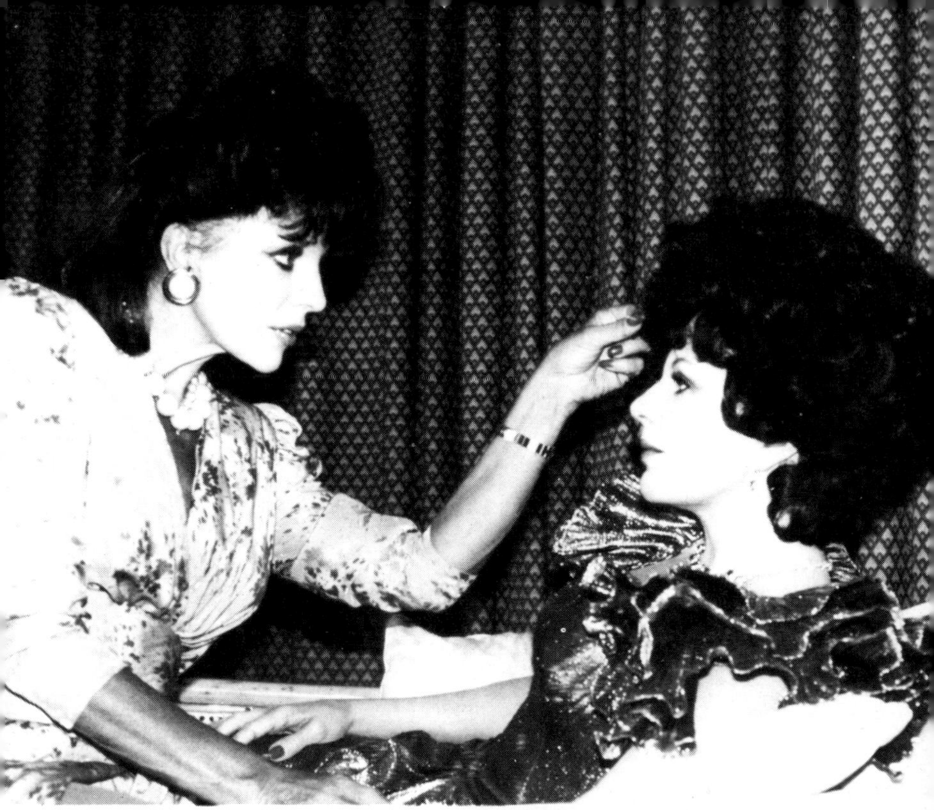

Joan comes face to face with her waxwork and makes some final adjustments to the hair.
(*Courtesy Madame Tussaud's, London*)

Joan prior to Holmlessness in May 1986.
(*AP/Wide World Photos*)

Joan testifying in court against her former husband, Peter Holm, in California, 1987.
(*AP/Wide World Photos*)

Jackie the novelist: the face that fits millions of book jackets.
(*AP/Wide World Photos*)

Joan's final farewell: leaving the family home in London with son Sacha to attend her father's funeral, April 1988. (*AP/Wide World Photos*)

A day at the golf course with boyfriend Bill Wiggins in England, 1987. (*AP/Wide World Photos*)

drummed up, Jackie was then quick to declare: "I don't write about anyone in particular."

One certainty is that ex-Swedish rocker, Peter Holm, is not a character. Holm, her sister Joan's ex, did not even make it into *Hollywood Husbands,* though he reportedly told Jackie he recognized himself as the guy with the heart of gold who gets involved with a TV star. "Peter," Jackie says she told him, "if it was you, it would have been a whole different story."

When Jackie began *Rock Star,* just as with previous novels, she says she had no idea what was going to happen. "I had no idea when Kris Phoenix started off at sixteen washing windows that he was going to end up with a gorgeous blonde and a million-dollar mansion."

She sums up: "So when I begin to write, it is an exciting trip for me. I think people are fascinated by how rock stars got there. How did Boy George get there? Sting? They all started as schoolboys with a guitar dream—the great rock 'n' roll dream. When you look back to Eric Clapton, the Animals, David Bowie; that's the sort of thing I wanted to capture."

A lesson, she adds further, inheres in the story. "I think it will tell people about the rock business," Jackie claims. "About what it takes to be a superstar. And I think it will teach kids what they have to do if they want to follow their dream." But Jackie hastens to add that her novels are intended as entertainment: "I want people to pick up a book and have a good time and forget about the headlines of the day and just read."

Her novels, she says, are as much an adventure for Jackie Collins as her readers. As part of the research for this book, she went on the road with a rock band. Typically, she will not reveal which one. Further, she read every book she could find on the rock-music industry. What she discovered was shocking—even to her: "I mean, in this day of AIDS and God-knows-what, they are still picking up the girls." AIDS gets a mention in the last chapters of this ever-contemporary author's work.

In one uncharacteristically personal, if not vaguely autobiographical, moment in the novel, Kris Phoenix's young son ends up comatose after a car crash. Jackie's niece, Katy (Joan's daughter), also went into a coma after an auto accident. No doubt, those agony-wrenching weeks worrying about Katy became a point of reference for the near-tragedy in the novel.

Rock Star is otherwise clearly not an autobiographical work. "Composites" is the word the author favors to describe her characters. As it happened, much of what Jackie discovered this time was quite foreign to her own existence. "I'm a moralist," she insists. "Nobody would believe a thirteen-year-old having sex with a roadie just to say hello to Mick Jagger. I couldn't write the whole truth because it was too unbelievable." Some of the details seemed far-fetched enough to prompt one interviewer to ask Jackie about her own imagination. "There is a very famous rock star who in real life was held by his ankles from a New York penthouse window," Jackie responded, "until he signed the legal papers." She added: "I remember Ringo saying to me that once he went to this Washington political dinner and that everyone was coming up saying, 'My husband is working tomorrow.' He could have had ninety-five percent of the women in the room. It was true. Famous men really can have most women."

Rock stars, she suggests, are loath to marry. "I think a lot of them reach the point where they have no respect for women," Jackie says, "because too many women are available to them. And even though it might be better for them personally, they don't really want to get married because it's not good for their image." As she told the *New York Post:* "A single rock star is much sexier than a married one. Of course, it's okay if they marry someone like Christie Brinkley because she's very glamorous herself, and fans like a glamorous couple coming together. But if he marries a nice little girl, all the other girls out there who want his body are thinking, 'That bitch, why wasn't it me?' "

Jackie also believes that one of the chief reasons fans are so attracted to rock stars is the proximity to them. "When you go to the movies," she explains, "you sit in the dark, and Paul Newman or Robert Redford or Tom Cruise is a fantasy figure up on the screen. But at a rock concert he's there in the flesh. There's an instant connection." Describing that connection, Jackie says, "The girls sit up front, they do their hair really prettily and are wearing their tight T-shirts. They hope that the rock star will notice them and the roadie will give them a backstage pass. It's a fantasy that can come true. If there's a wife involved, it's not such a fantasy."

Such pathetic little girls never cut it as main characters in her novels. "I like writing strong women," she admits. "They take initiative. They want independence and a lot out of life. They're not nymphos or hookers—well, not my main characters. They're very positive women. They're like Lucky. I always have one positive character that women love." Certainly the three women in *The Love Killers* are a good example. They take on a powerful Mafia family to avenge the death of a woman activist who was trying to stamp out prostitution. And in *The World Is Full of Divorced Women* a good-looking celebrity journalist opts for her career instead of another marriage.

Hype as much as hard work goes into the making of her blockbusters. Once a book is launched, Jackie hits the talk-show circuit. No interview, it seems, is too small for her to do. But she does have one requirement—that there be little or no mention of her sister Joan. She is, by all accounts, totally devoted to her craft, and more than willing to talk about writing. As one journalist observed, "Jackie gets into her writing with delighted gusto." So much so that it sometimes rankles, but more often intrigues, Jackie when people say, "I'm going to write a Jackie Collins novel, and I'll put sex on page twenty, thirty, and forty, and those are the ingredients." But, counters an incredulous Jackie, "I don't have any ingredients."

Her book tours are transatlantic, and she is a talk-show host's dream guest. On one program in England, the Wogan show, she got caught in what might be called a battle of the best-selling authors. Romance novelist Barbara Cartland, appearing alongside Jackie, told her in no uncertain terms that her books are "evil and promote bad and perverse ideas in young people." Undaunted, Jackie, coolly and graciously, responded, "I think there's room for both of us."

Though Barbara Cartland says she liked Jackie as a person, she still cannot say anything nice about her books. "I think her books are wicked, disgusting, and vulgar," she told us. "Especially in this day and age when we should be promoting a return to morality." But, adds Cartland, "I also find Harold Robbins horrible. I threw his books away, too." What mostly concerns her is the effect of such books on young people. "It's not just because I'm old," Cartland explains. "But young people remember those perverse descriptions. Even if you try to forget them, you will remember. It's very dangerous."

Apparently some seventy-five million people around the globe do not agree with Cartland. This is the number of people who read the novels of Jackie Collins. They include some of Hollywood's rich and famous. "I love her," says Angie Dickinson, "but that doesn't mean I trust her. I mean she'll take notes right in front of me."

Alana Hamilton Stewart, ex-wife of both George Hamilton and Rod Stewart, admits to telling Collins too many intimate details of her life. "I trust her completely to change the names so I'll be safe," she says. "Otherwise I'll kill her." Jackie also counts Whitney Houston among her fans. "I had the pleasure of meeting Whitney at the Grammy Awards parties in New York," Jackie says. "And she said she reads my books. I told her I love her records."

In or out of the limelight, each and every one of her readers, according to Jackie, matters to her. "I had one woman say to me, 'You know, you really saved my marriage,'" Jackie revealed to one television interviewer. "'I read *Hollywood Husbands* and there were things in that that really saved my marriage.'" One of the more bizarre, but no less flattering reactions to her novels came during a suit Jackie filed against a magazine that wrongly identified her in nude photographs they published. Jackie won a judgment of ten million dollars, but lost one of her fans during jury selection. "She was reading a book of mine called *Chances*," Jackie recounts. "And the judge said to her 'You know you are reading this book by Miss Collins, and this case is coming up, and you know you'll have to stop reading it.'"

The would-be juror, according to Collins, gave her own verdict. "I can't do that," the woman told the judge, who promptly disqualified her from the jury. "Too bad," she said. "I'm going home to read."

Ultimately, the award would be overturned by a higher court on the ground that the defendant had not acted with malice.

Jackie Collins says that she wants to be judged by future generations as someone who wrote books that reflected a particular time. If they should detect some sex and scandal in her works, according to Collins, "That's just because I was re-writing what happens daily in Hollywood."

For now Jackie ranks among the publishing in-dustry's quartet of best-selling novelists that in-cludes Stephen King, Sydney Sheldon, and Danielle Steele. Though Jackie has also earned the labels "Queen of Flash and Trash" and "Someone Who Writes Blueprints for Miniseries," there are some academics in her corner. One of them is Pro-fessor Toth of Pennsylvania State University, who argues that Jackie Collins plays an important part in contemporary literature. "She has a strong imagination, strong plots, and just as Shakespeare did in his day, a certain support of traditional val-ues. And, what's more, she has a very good under-standing of what people want to read."

Inarguably, the sale figures testify to the profes-sor's last point. Shortly after the publication of *Rock Star* and a marathon of promotional dates, Doubleday's main Fifth Avenue store in New York was selling on average twenty copies an hour.

There are some who ask about why Jackie Col-lins does not write a more serious book. It was Jackie Collins herself who once remarked, "Could I write Frederick Forsyth's books? Could he write mine? No!"

Why should Jackie Collins, so famous for her leopard-skin prints, change her spots?

Hollywood Knives

When Joan Collins returned to Hollywood in the late sixties, she was Mrs. Anthony Newley, and also the mother of two children.

Almost from her first glance at Newley in August 1962, while having lunch with a friend in London's trendy White Elephant, Joan seemed destined to play second fiddle to his career. Though still gun-shy with men after Beatty, Joan found herself in-trigued by this full-cheeked Cockney chap, with his thick brown hair, alert eyes, and a rather promi-nent nose that she would describe, euphemisti-cally, as "Romanesque." She observed further his "satanic and intense" look and "beautifully expres-sive hands," always in motion during his conversa-tions. Newley, seated at the next table with his partner Leslie Bricusse, was the talk of the town then. *Stop the World—I Want to Get Off*, in which he played sort of an Everyman, a quite short, al-most clownish figure, registering the gamut of hu-man experience, was an enormous success. Newley had, with Bricusse, also directed and written the book, music, and lyrics for the show.

A few weeks later, her friend, actor Robert Wag-ner, who was in London making a film, took her to the show. Joan remembers being both drained and exhilarated by Newley's performance. They went backstage after the show to Newley's dressing room and ended up all having dinner together. By night's end, Joan was absolutely smitten with

Newley. She was thrilled to hear from a friend at lunch later that week how taken Newley was with her beauty and that he wanted her phone number. But the clincher, it seemed, was that, according to this mutual friend, Tony, then in his late twenties, had never been in love. Joan seized on this tidbit of information as a challenge. Of course, this was hardly a secret revelation since the most memorable song of Newley's show, "What Kind of Fool Am I?" was a philosophical lament about what kind of fool Little Chap, Newley's character, is for never loving before.

Duly infatuated, Joan began to date Tony and—kiss those lyrics good-bye—soon he professed his love for her.

Trouble was, Newley was separated from his first wife and thus unable to marry Joan just then. Several months later he admitted to an affair upon Joan's discovery of it. They split briefly after *Stop the World—I Want to Get Off* opened in New York, but made up about a week later on a park bench in Central Park. They promptly moved into a penthouse together in the East Sixties. And six weeks later Joan was pregnant. On October 12, 1963, a daughter, Tara, was born to the couple who married just in time—a day before the birth—for Tony to be the legal father. Less than two years later, on September 8, 1965, Joan gave birth to a son, Alexander Anthony (Sacha) Newley.

It was just as well that she could perform these domestic roles because there seemed to be few acting roles bestowed upon her. Now well into her thirties and with some fairly forgettable movies on her résumé to date, she got a chilly reception around the Hollywood studios. Even in the commissary at Twentieth Century-Fox, which had brought her to America back in the fifties and put her under contract to them, she was barely noticed.

Not only had the contract system virtually disappeared, but there was also a whole new crop of stars now. Among them: Candice Bergen, Julie Christie, Barbra Streisand, and Faye Dunaway. The beauteous Joan, living mostly in London and New York in recent years, was not included in this all-star cast.

This time it was her husband whom Fox, her former employer, brought to Hollywood to star in *Doctor Doolittle.* Joan had hoped to get a part in the film, but even with Newley's clout, was turned down. Now, four years into her marriage with Newley, Joan faced the dreary prospect of playing the role of a housewife, albeit in a Beverly Hills home with a swimming pool. Almost echoing the theme of Betty Friedan's major work, *The Feminine Mystique,* she despaired, "The truth is, I enjoy working—why do I feel pangs of guilt when I admit it?"

In later years, describing that period of her life, Joan sounded like she was quoting from the pages of sister Jackie's *Hollywood Wives.* "Why wasn't I content, like most of the Beverly Hills matrons I knew, to be a faithful wife (albeit ignored) and a dutiful mother?" Joan wrote in her autobiography. "Content to run the house with my trusty Portuguese couple, to lie by the pool and ruin my skin, and then go to the facialist and the dermatologist to repair it, go to the analyst, the hairdresser, the manicurist, the gynecologist, the numerologist, the group therapy session, the tennis lessons, the tap-dancing classes, the kaffee klatches, the hen-party lunches, the backgammon classes, the beach and the gym . . . Apart from the above, there was always shopping."

In a sense Joan had made her own bed. But true

to her character she would not lie in it for long. She had met Newley back in London just after completing work on *The Road to Hong Kong*. Her costars in this film were Bob Hope, whom she found "consistently charming, warm and down-to-earth," and Bing Crosby, who was often "offhand, grumpy, vague." He also had rancid breath, which she inhaled during a kissing scene. But her main reason for accepting the role had been to finally sever her relationship with ex-fiancé Warren Beatty. The film allowed her to return to London, where, away from Warren and totally in charge of her life, she might resuscitate her ailing career. One of the few movies Joan did in her early days with Newley was *La Conguintura* in Portofino and Lugano. It was her first separation from Tony, and she took their baby girl, Tara, on location with her. Then Hollywood beckoned—Tony.

Once back there, Joan instantly recognized how her star had fallen. Meanwhile, she was finding it increasingly difficult to get much attention from her husband who had a boundless passion for work. About this time Joan was, by her own admission, starting to wonder "What kind of fool am I," from the title of one of Newley's show-stopping tunes.

She had, after all, paid her dues in Hollywood. That few, if any, seemed to remember was worse than a stab in the back. In part, it was also because a new breed of executive was now in place. Nonetheless, indifference could kill a career as effectively, if not more so, than a direct cut. Yet Joan did not give up hope. She took whatever work was available. She would start all over again with no guarantee that she could ever surface again as a star.

Reduced now to the small instead of the silver screen, she had some parts in TV series like *The*

Man from U.N.C.L.E., Batman, Mission Impossible and *Star Trek*. She livened up her nights by going to the Daisy, a disco that reminded her of the lively scene back in London. Together with, among others, Paul Newman, Sammy Davis, Jr., and Peter Lawford, she and Newley later opened their own disco, the Factory, at that point more "in" in Hollywood than Joan. The place drew an array of celebrities: Barbra Streisand, Bobby Kennedy, Peter Sellers, Dean Martin, to name just a few. In a year, the Factory faded from popularity, just like Joan's Hollywood career.

What Joan hoped would rescue her from a crumbling career, and now marriage, was a new film that consumed vast amounts of Newley's time as a writer, director and star. The film, *Can Hieronymous Merkin Ever Forget Mercy Humppe and Find Happiness*, was meant to be an erotic musical comedy. But it left Joan feeling unhappy and dejected. First, she was denied the female lead, and also she was hurt by Merkin's (Newley's alter-ego) philandering. At that point, she realized her career and marriage were falling apart.

Joan acted in some celluloid films in Spain and Italy. The Italian director of *State of Siege* told Joan it was an intellectual film. She ended up in the role of a desperate young widow involved with a seventeen-year-old boy. The script also called for Joan to do a nude scene. The movie was made in Trieste.

Before packing up and returning to Britain, Joan appeared in a comedy, *Up in the Cellar* (*Three in the Cellar*), with Larry Hagman, who one day would be known as J.R. in Dallas. Back home Joan did not fare much better. With such flicks as *Fear in the Night, Tales From the Crypt,* and *Dark Places,* the actress who was once known as "Britain's Bad

Girl" was graduated by the press to "Queen of Horror Films."

By the early seventies she was divorced and had a new husband and a third child. Joan's marriage to Newley lasted as long as it did, seven years, because of the children. Joan worried about the effect divorce would have on them. However, by 1970, they both agreed that there was no way to repair the marriage, which had been sundered by Newley's wandering eye and, above all, the glaring differences in their personalities. While Joan was outgoing and extroverted, Tony was more a homebody and introverted. Joan respected and loved Tony but felt they could not survive as a couple.

As the Newley marriage was reaching its finale in 1970, along came Ron Kass, a thirty-three-year-old American who was president of the Beatles' Apple Records and recently separated from his wife. He came along to dinner at a King's Road Italian restaurant-disco with Joan and Tony; Eva Bricusse, the wife of Tony's partner; and Doug Hayward, who was tailor to both Newley and Kass. Joan remembers being instantly attracted to Kass, who radiated charm and energy. The quirkiness that characterized actors, producers, and playboys who buzzed around Joan seemed to be absent from his personality. There was a solidity to this man. This quality, along with the dazzling green eyes set inside a deeply tanned and handsome face, proved a powerful attraction. Kass not only had a master's degree in business from UCLA, but also a degree in music, and was quite accomplished at the trombone.

Kass also checked out well in the astrological department. Like Sydney Chaplin and Warren Beatty, her former boyfriends, Kass was not only an Aries, but incredibly, was born on the same day, March 30, as both of them. Kass handled his work artfully and zestfully, crisscrossing continents on business and never seeming to tire. During this first dinner, it would be Tony who tired of company and wanted only to go home, which he did, to be alone with his work. Joan stayed on long into the night talking to Kass who obviously was as taken with her as she with him.

At first Joan and Kass would meet for lunch and tea in London, and then Los Angeles, where Kass also had an office. By then, Tony and Joan had an unspoken agreement that they would go separate ways. With the divorce finalized, Joan moved with her two children back to London where Ron was now heading MGM Records. She took her own flat in order to ease the children into their new life in London without the added complication of getting a new daddy. Tony, according to their mutual agreement, was entitled to see the children as frequently as he liked.

Ever the romantic, Joan did not want to ruin her love affair with Kass by getting married. Her previous track record was another factor in this decision. But by 1972 Joan married Kass, and on June 20 of that year Katyana Kass was born. A Gemini like Joan, Katy would have a special bond with her mother. "She and I," Joan once wrote, "probably understand each other better than anyone else in the world."

Joan put the horror films behind her and did, among other projects, a prestigious NBC-TV Hallmark Hall of Fame two-hour special, *The Man Who Came to Dinner*. Shot in England, the special would air in America at Thanksgiving. Joan played the flamboyant and eccentric Lorraine Sheldon, a part she found to be a delight. Were it not for the legendary actor, Orson Welles, starring in it, the work, too, would have also been a pleasure. But Joan remembers him being both contentious and tyrannical, virtually taking over everyone else's role by instructing them at every turn how to act. Though *The Man Who Came to Dinner* was an excellent credit for Joan, it got poor ratings. But the widow of the play's author, the late Moss Hart, gave Joan some cause to celebrate. On a visit to the set, according to Joan, Kitty Carlisle Hart told her that she was the best Lorraine Sheldon ever.

In 1975, after some five years of what she regarded as one of the happiest periods of her life, Joan came back to Hollywood a third time. The tax situation in England dictated that they leave England to preserve their money. Ron, who had lived in London for more than ten years, was insistent on moving. Joan, finally getting known again as a British film star and, more importantly, preferring life in London, was heartbroken. Ron, who now had an excellent job as president of Warner Brothers Records in London, left to head a new film company called Sagittarius in Los Angeles. Sagittarius was the creation of Edgar Bronfman; heir to the Seagram whiskey fortune. Kass was more than a business friend of Bronfman; he once flew to New York to comfort Bronfman, who was awaiting word on the fate of his kidnapped son, Sam. On a happier occasion, the mogul Bronfman would turn to Ron and Joan to throw a big birthday bash for his son Edgar, Jr., on his turning 21. Weeks went into preparing the party, which was attended by the crème de la crème of Hollywood (a guest list very much Joan and Ron's doing), and which went on until two o'clock in the morning—rather extraordinary in a town that turns in and gets up early.

The afternoon after the party, while Joan was luxuriating in compliments from guests that had arrived all day in the form of phone calls, notes and flowers, Ron arrived home to tell her

Bronfman had fired him. No reason, according to
Joan, was ever given. Bronfman paid Kass off until
the end of the month. Now Kass, the major breadwinner, was out of work.

The Kasses were left with an enormous mort-
gage on a hugely expensive house, and three children who were just getting used to schools. "I was
bitterly resentful of Edgar Bronfman," Joan wrote
in her autobiography. "I had never in my life been
bitter and resentful toward anyone, but now the
major breadwinner of the Kass family was out of
work. . . . I don't think Ron ever fully recovered
from the traumatic disappointment, pain and
shock that Edgar caused him. Certainly this became a turning point in our lives up until now."
The Kasses moved to a smaller house and with the
profits from the sale of the house managed, according to Ron, to live in the style to which they were
accustomed. Joan didn't agree.

With a husband out of work and still trying to
get past the devastating blow dealt him, it was left
to Joan to take on the role of sole breadwinner.
From the Newley divorce she had not asked for
alimony, only child support. During that marriage
she had been virtually bankrupt of major roles and
the salaries that went with them. Thus she was not
in particularly good financial shape. Kass had
three sons by a previous marriage to worry about.
Now somewhat down and out in Beverly Hills,
Joan was motivated more by survival than anything else. For the moment she packed away her
dreams of stardom. She did some more celluloid
movie jobs, for $10,000 to $15,000, and got some
bit parts in television series.

Joan would experience a dramatic comedown
when she had hoped for a comeback. First came
Starsky and Hutch in Hawaii, in which she had a
bit part. On location she confessed her despair to a

tabloid photographer. Remarkably, the photographer did not violate Joan's confidence. Still, her self-esteem must have reached an all-time low then if she made a quasi-confidant of someone whom she would have avoided under other circumstances. She accepted a small part in a TV movie, *The Moneychangers*, for a mere $5,000, less than she was earning a week in the last two years under contract with Fox.

The Moneychangers led, ironically, to a somewhat grand entrance at the Santa Monica Unemployment Office. Having just come from the opening of an English boutique on Sunset Boulevard, where she had acted as hostess, Joan pulled into the driveway of the Unemployment building in a gold Mercedes. Her secretary had suggested Santa Monica rather than Hollywood on the theory that Joan would not be as instantly recognizable at that locale.

Though fast becoming an unknown around the Hollywood studios, Joan *was*, along with her Mercedes, something of a celebrity at Unemployment. She fled in total humiliation. "Suddenly the realization came to me that I wasn't getting any younger," she remembers thinking, "and I certainly wasn't getting any more successful. With the children soon going off to college, I'd better do something rather than wait for my agent to call with an offer to do *Fantasy Island.*"

But there would be one more job in Hollywood before she departed for England in 1978 where, it seemed, a woman over forty was not discarded as in Hollywood. Joan Collins would ultimately become a cult figure there. And Kass would help mastermind a publicity campaign to champion the over-forty woman. To Joan's thinking, her Hollywood finale was the lowest point of her career. "The film was *Empire of the Ants,*" she recalls. "The title tells it all. I went off to the Florida swamps before Christmas. And I played the role of a woman who gets lost in the jungle and is terrorized by these giant man-eating seven-foot papier-mâché ants. And we had to be in the swamps. I was in the swamps up to my knees wearing boots, and we had to fall in. My legs were covered with cuts—they were all infected. And it was really the lowest point of my life."

Clearly, the only way to go now was up. And Joan, forty-four, was more determined than ever to get there.

Jackie to the Rescue

In a sense it was little sister Jackie who rescued Joan from the unemployment line, worldwide obscurity, and the possibility of turning into a pathetic party joke. Jackie would give Joan an option on her book, *The Stud,* as a film in which she would star as the disco doyenne Fontaine Khaled, and then make its sequel, *The Bitch.*

Wanting to have some control over her career, Joan decided that she should buy her own film properties. This posed a problem because of her financial situation. Instead she would rely on family ties, namely Jackie's talents. However, the task of engaging a backer fell on Joan, who, in her own words, "schlepped" the project all over Hollywood and elsewhere in search of a taker.

Joan Collins had paid her dues in Hollywood. Over almost three decades in show business she had been a minor star, appearing in forgettable films and all-too-uninspiring television shows, including *Batman, Police Women, Starsky and Hutch, Mission Impossible,* and the like. But despite her experience in the industry, getting *The Stud* made was proving to be quite a feat.

Getting nowhere with it in Hollywood, Joan started looking abroad. Fortuitously, she was at the Cannes Film Festival promoting *Empire of the Ants* when she met British producer George Walker of the Brent Walker film group. She showed him Jackie's screenplay, and he liked it enough to back it. Husbands Kass and Lerman signed on as coproducers.

Joan was given a reported $30,000 to star in *The Stud*. It would be her raunchiest role to date. "It was preferable to *Empire of the Ants* because to have a giant papier-mâché ant fall on top of you and kill you with its noxious fumes is the most embarrassing and awful thing an actress can do," Joan once said. "I decided I would take off my clothes and do *The Stud*. I'd rather do porno than ants."

The film would eventually become a cult movie of the seventies. It earned about forty million dollars. At last Joan, with the help of Jackie's prose, was back in the big time. This time, though, she was determined to stay there. Though the film got largely unfavorable reviews, at least Joan found herself a hot media item once again. Said *The New York Times*: "*The Stud* is an ugly soft-core pornographic account of the rise and fall of a fancy man. It is illiterate and anti-erotic. The performances, Quentin Masters' direction and cinematography and editing are all amateurish."

People magazine spotlighted Joan: "If you miss one movie this year, make sure this is it. Joan Collins, debasing herself as few actresses of substance have done, plays a London nightclub owner who is so tired of her rich older husband that she throws her clothes off whenever the title character even gets near her neighborhood. At 46, she still has an attractive body, but displays it with such insistent regularity that she seems more ludicrous than sensuous. The script is, to be generous, slimy, vulgar and stupid."

Its sequel was *The Bitch*, which, with hindsight, Joan admits to exploiting herself in.

The Bitch finds Fontaine a divorcée with her disco, Hobo, in serious financial trouble. In the beginning of the story, Fontaine remains randy as ever, even bedding her young chauffeur once. Later she puts all her energies into saving the disco. But ultimately she meets her match in Nico Constantine, a handsome Greek, widowed by a wealthy older woman, who loses his inheritance to casinos, and now is deep in debt to the Mob. Fontaine and the irresistibly handsome and charming Nico have met their match in each other. Together at a horse race, they both go for broke and ultimately find out the truth about each other.

Along with the notoriety of both *The Stud* and its sequel *The Bitch* came Joan's 1978 autobiography *Past Imperfect*, which became an instant bestseller. Once again, Joan had some serious reservations about how she had cast herself.

Past Imperfect caused such an uproar in England that Joan, according to *Playboy*, demurely returned a hundred-thousand-dollar advance to Warner Books to keep the autobiography from being published in America. Or, as Joan herself explained to *People* in a November 1979 profile, "I've changed," she said of the frank exposé. "People might think I'm like that." Joan also figured that she would be slaughtered by critics here, as well. But later, after all the press attention from *Dynasty* focused on her, rumors about the book's having been banned began to make tongues wag here. To counteract that myth, Joan decided to update, rewrite, and edit the English version for its U.S. publication. The hardcover appeared in the spring of 1984 by Simon and Schuster, was reviewed favorably, and stayed on the best-seller list, eventually making the No. 2 spot for three months. A year later, in 1985, it came out in paperback, published by Berkley.

Her dubious exposure in both films had also resulted in the highly successful Cinzano aperitif advertising campaign. Joan, as the calm and collected Melissa, became a regular face on British television. In the commercial, Joan suffered the clumsy antics of a buffoon, played by the late Leonard Rossiter, who figures himself a bon vivant. She brought a certain insouciant wit to her part. One commercial had Cinzano dripping down on her navel only moments after she had arranged herself meticulously on a chaise longue for some relaxing sunbathing.

Although Joan says that she has no real regrets about the way she has lived her life, in her autobiography she talks about some of her misgivings. A major one was the film title, *The Bitch*. As Joan put it: "They gave it a damn-awful exploitative title, which stuck to me like fly paper through the popular press for years." She recalls how she begged Brent-Walker not to use the title. As it turned out, her pleas were to no avail.

From her point of view the release of *The Bitch* was premature. Among the problems, according to her, were an unfinished script and the casting of an unknown Italian actor as her leading man. Though both sisters' husbands, Kass and Lerman, were again involved in this venture, even they could not persuade Brent-Walker Limited to change the title or script.

Yet it gave Joan's career a tremendous boost in terms of exposure, albeit not exactly the type she sought, and opened up another market for her. By 1980, Joan Collins, film and television actress, came in video cassette, too. Advertisements for the video teased, "Give your boyfriend Joan Collins for Christmas."

The film's publicity blurb read: "This naughty adventure bears elements of a caper and it's set in the lush surroundings of society's glossiest, naughtiest playgrounds—liberally laced with eroticism and spiced with witty double entendres, it's a combination that makes it absolutely for adults only."

Despite its enormous commercial success, *The Bitch*, as far as Joan was concerned, was nothing more than sheer exploitation. At least *The Stud* had been something of a campy romp, but there was no defense for *The Bitch*. The final humiliation came at the 1979 Cannes Film Festival. As Joan relaxed on the Brent-Walker yacht with, among other friends, actor Kirk Douglas, a light aircraft with a banner buzzed overhead. The banner proclaiming "Joan Collins Is The Bitch," sailed across the skies of the Côte d'Azur in full view of all the movers and shakers in the film industry. Quite understandably, Joan was blazing mad. In years to follow, Joan and her partners would file a multi-million-dollar suit against Brent-Walker Ltd. for alleged fraud, conspiracy, and breach of contract over royalty payments from *The Stud*. The film group made an interim settlement, in 1986, of £147,233, and an independent account of profits from the film to determine how much more was owed them, in return for Joan and her co-plaintiffs' dropping the suit. Incredibly, Joan's salary for the film had been a mere £25,000.

Despite her despair over the film, Joan would ultimately profit from it in a way that she never could have imagined then. Joan as the bitchy disco doyenne Fontaine Khaled was *Dynasty*'s Alexis Carrington in the making.

Executive producer Aaron Spelling, the king of glitzy soaps and made-for-TV movies, as well as the series *Charlie's Angels*, approached masterminds Richard and Esther Shapiro to help him craft a show that would be a rival to the hit *Dallas*. "We wanted an oil-based family and chose Denver," Esther says, "because we like writing about Middle America." And so *Dynasty* was born.

The show that was broadcast for the first time on January 12, 1981, has since become one of the most successful prime-time soap operas in the history of television. In its infancy, *Dynasty*, like any new show, had to find and build its audience. Further, a character with the bite of Dallas's "J.R." was crucial to making the show a hit. Alexis, as played by Joan Collins, fitted the bill perfectly. Her first appearance on *Dynasty* not only lifted the ratings, but also virtually sent them through the roof. As with *Dallas*, the money in *Dynasty* came from oil. The distinguished silver-haired actor, John Forsythe, played her ex-husband, Blake Carrington, in the series. Previously, among his many other roles, Forsthye was the voice of private detective Charlie in *Charlie's Angels*.

Blake Carrington ran his vast holdings from an opulent, forty-eight-room mansion. When the series started, however, his empire was on the brink of collapse because of problems in the Middle East. There was also trouble on the home front.

Among his problems: his current wife and former secretary, Krystle, played by Linda Evans, complained about being treated like one of his many possessions. The troubles of other characters were even less dramatic, posing a problem with the series itself. Fallon, then played by Pamela Sue Martin, was just a spoiled daughter. Steven, Blake's homosexual son, had plastic surgery after an accident. All the accident and surgery that followed achieved was to let the actor Al Corley leave the show, to be replaced by Jack Coleman.

With the first season of *Dynasty* drawing to a close, the ratings were not making the dent in *Dallas* that Spelling had expected from the series. The production team looked once again at *Dallas* to figure out what might be the missing element in *Dynasty*. The success of *Dallas* was due in large part to J.R. Ewing, the richest villain on television. By contrast, during *Dynasty*'s first season, there was action, amour, and glamour, but no real villain.

Blake Carrington showed signs of villainy by killing his son Steven's lover, Ted Diamond, and having to stand trial. But there was confusion in the minds of viewers because the killing had been, after all, an accident. Worse, Blake and Krystle appeared to the audience to be almost too good to be true. What was needed rather urgently was a cliff-hanger last show to lure viewers into watching next season, and also pump up the ratings.

Understandably, the final episode took much time to prepare. Blake was to testify under oath that Ted Diamond's death was an accident and, most importantly, that he loved his son Steven. Spelling's trump card was the surprise witness to be called by the prosecution. That surprise witness would be none other than Blake's ex-wife, who had vanished from his life years before. Now, the woman—who had deserted her own children—would resurface as the ace witness against Blake.

Thus began Spelling and the Shapiros' search for the perfect actress to play this mysterious witness. Originally they thought they would name her Madeline, but they decided instead on Alexis, which had more bite. For the final episode of the first season, they used a stand-in actress, camouflaging her in a white suit, a hat, and a veil, and had her photographed in a way that would not reveal any part of her face. The hunt for Alexis was now underway in earnest. The audience was finally hooked. Who would the mysterious witness turn out to be?

Enter Joan Collins. Though Sophia Loren, Elizabeth Taylor, and Raquel Welch were all under consideration, it was Joan Collins who ranked on the top of Esther Shapiro's list. But Esther had to per-

suade others. So convinced was she that Joan was
right for the part, she held out for her.

"Joan was older," says Shapiro, "and the reaction
was strong against her. People felt her accent
would not be understood and they thought she was
over the hill." But Shapiro stuck to her guns. "I
thought she was the only person for the role. She
has humor, and Alexis had to be—and Joan is—a
great beauty."

Esther Shapiro made the right choice, and Joan
would never forget the day she got the call about
the part of Alexis. She was on holiday at the time in
Marbella, Spain. Several versions of the conversation between Joan and her agent Tom Korman
have been reported since. One appears in the book,
TV Babylon, by author Jeff Rovin. In a chapter entitled "Joan Collins: The Ultimate TV Bitch," he reveals: "When Collins's agent phoned to tell her
about the TV role, among the first words out of his
mouth was, 'She's a bitch.' He apparently knew
where his client's bread was buttered, and so did
she. Having seen that that kind of role was the key
to public acceptance, Collins agreed to take the
part." By her own account, Korman rang up and
asked if she had heard of *Dynasty.* To which she
answered with a question: "No, never—what's *Dynasty?*"

Soon she would find out. And once she did, there
was no question in her mind that she wanted the
part.

But there was a problem in her path. Joan was
under contract to London's Triumph Productions
for a two-week run of the play *Murder In Mind.*
She was worried about the possibility of a suit
should she pull out of her commitment. At the
same time, though she had trained in theater and
had an abiding affection for it, she thought her career was in the doldrums at that moment. Her for-

mer RADA classmate Gerald Harper remembers a
visit she paid to him in his dressing room at a West
End theater where he was appearing in a successful thriller, *House Guest.* He remembers Joan telling him, "The only job I've got is a thriller touring
the provinces. It's a terrible play."

Harper says he was delighted that, next thing,
Joan was in *Dynasty* instead of what he called a
second-rate thriller. "In my book, what I really like
about her is that she's got guts, and she just gets up
and does it." In his view Joan was brave to accept
the *Dynasty* offer, a major role in television, where
previously she had had only small parts. This did
not surprise Harper, who also praises her for having the courage previously to star, in 1980, in a
festival theater production of *The Last of Mrs. Che-
ney.* "She hadn't been on stage for many years," he
recalls. "Even Dirk Bogarde said he was too terrified and stopped. But Joan just sauntered on and
did it. I have great admiration for that."

Joan stood firm on her desire to do *Dynasty* and
emerged with her reputation unscathed by breaking the theater contract. She knew that this was an
opportunity that could change her life. But she did
not exactly saunter onto the set of *Dynasty.* Of her
first day, Joan remembers, "I was certainly nervous. It was mid-August 1981, ninety degrees in the
shade. I was surrounded by strange faces of the
crew and cast, some friendly, some noncommittal.
I had to prove myself. To them I was some British
broad come over to take America by storm."

Prove herself she did, and during her first season
as Alexis, she gave *Dallas*'s J.R. a run for his money
for the title of all-time TV villain. At ex-husband
Blake's trial, she tries to demolish his nice-guy image by revealing that he paid her off, to the tune of
two hundred fifty thousand dollars a year, to keep
away from their children. In another show there is

an infamous scene where Alexis's fiancé, Cecil Colby, also an oil tycoon, suffers a heart attack while making love to her. Slapping the heart attack victim on the face to at least keep her dreams of inheriting all his money alive, Alexis implores, "Don't you dare die on me, Cecil! You can't die on me. I need you to get Blake." Once Cecil is rushed to a hospital, a determined Alexis manages to marry him on his deathbed.

Now, several years into the show, there have been few episodes in which Alexis has not either committed adultery, coveted someone else's husband, poisoned someone's mind, gotten even with Blake, sniped at Krystle, or all of the above. On a really quiet day in Denver, she may merely lie and cheat and lust after someone. In fact, as England's *Daily Telegraph* pointed out, Alexis is not alone in her evil deeds. *"Dynasty's* cast attempt murder, kidnap and rape and try to steal each other's money." Only, it seems, Alexis is the best at it. There are, however, some guidelines that even she must obey. They come from network television censors who limit the amount of smoking and drinking allowed during each episode.

Some people allege that Alexis's character spills over into Joan's private life. One of them was her late ex-husband Ron Kass who was quoted as saying, "Joan is superb as the superbitch in *Dynasty,* and she was just as good in the role when we were together at home." Their daughter Katy disagrees vehemently. "Mum has a great sense of humor," says Katy. "She's really outgoing and friendly."

Joan's friend, Douglas Hayward, agrees, saying that she, as well as Jackie, has a great sense of humor and, in sharp contrast to Alexis, is also fiercely loyal. About the only way he sees Alexis as the perfect character for Joan is career-wise. "I mean, if I were an actor," he says, "I'd want to do a really gutsy part. It's a much more glossy show card."

He remembers a party Joan gave back in the early seventies, almost a decade before *Dynasty*. One of the guests, according to Hayward, was behaving in an Alexis-like manner. "I was there, being seriously attacked by this woman," he recalls. "She was a very strong, tough woman, and nobody tackled with her. She said, 'Hayward, you're full of shit,' just as Joan walked by. Joan turned around and said, 'Hey, just a second. He's one of my close friends. And I don't want anyone talking to him like that in my house. Or out you go!' This took incredible courage. Joan gets points for this. It says something about loyalty."

Michael Alcock, the publishing director of England's Aurum Press, remembers Joan as a caring person. While editorial director at Macmillan, he worked directly with her on the *Joan Collins Beauty Book*. Unlike Alexis, draped in glamourous and extravagant Nolan Miller creations, Joan showed a particular sensitivity to the average woman. "She had very strong views about clothes for her book," Alcock says. "Although rich and famous herself, Joan had a very strong understanding of the ordinary woman's budget and thought that it was much better to have timeless, classic outfits than ephemeral fashions." He adds: "She was so friendly, so easy to work with. I once did a book with Raquel Welch who was far more difficult. Joan was always on time. She never canceled a meeting. It was her book, and she knew how to do it."

Joan has another view. "I think the facet the public is most familiar with is the in-control, slightly domineering, slightly assertive or aggressive, if you will, female," she says. "But that is not the way I am all the time. I have a certain amount of shyness which I think most actors do. I was very shy when I was a child. I think that could again be one of the reasons why the character I play on *Dynasty* is popular. Although she's painted as a daredevil, she has a side that is quite warm and vulnerable, and I think quite witty in a way."

Joan also defends against the notion that, perhaps, she has become Alexis in real life. "It's called acting," she says simply. "I based the character on a very good friend of mine who unfortunately died. She was a jet-setter, very amusing, very interested in men and power, but very liked by both men and women."

The part of Alexis Joan dislikes, she insists, is the very same part *Dynasty* writers like. "They're always writing these nasty things for her to do and saying how terrible she is," Joan reports. "Five years ago Alexis fired a gun at a pregnant Krystle who was on horseback." She adds, "I think Alexis is probably made to be more bitchy than her character demands."

Joan admits, though, that her delivery might add more bite to Alexis's barbs. Says Joan, whose clipped English accent was objected to by some people involved in *Dynasty:* "I think one of the things is the way I deliver the zingers sometimes. I deliver quite a lot of zingers, which I like to do."

While Joan gets vast exposure and mega-money, reportedly around ninety-five thousand dollars per episode, from *Dynasty,* she gives as much back in time and commitment to the show. As Joan told *People,* "I don't think people realize how tough it is . . . It's like making an eight-month movie, plus for a woman it's even harder. It's not shooting the show every day. In one season alone I have worn over 100 outfits and that means additional time for several fittings for each one. And women have to be on the lot a half hour or more before the men for makeup." On Sundays, she confesses, she gives her face a rest from the makeup. From her fair-skinned mother Elsa, she says, she learned how to take care of her skin. "Makeup protects the skin," she explains, "but it becomes destructive when people don't take it off properly and it clogs their pores."

Much as Joan likes to burn the candles at both ends, when she is working on *Dynasty*, she generally turns in by 8:30 or 9 P.M. with a box of biscuits, TV, and trash magazines that, in her own words, "provide stress control. You read them and think, 'You got problems?' "

During the *Dynasty* season Joan averages between five and seven hours of sleep a night. Otherwise she never sleeps more than nine or ten. Joan's description of the demanding, if not punishing, schedule, is echoed by former *Dynasty* cast member Diahann Carroll who played Dominique Deveraux, a black singer who gave Alexis a run for her money in the nastiness department. "The pressure is primarily on the women because of the hours," Carroll recalls of her own period on the show. "You had to get up very early, often at 3 A.M., in order to be in makeup and hair at 4:30 A.M. That's hard!"

Though there was the battle of the bitches on the set, Diahann found Joan to be quite the opposite of Alexis off it. "We get on very well," she said at the time. "If there was anything in particular that was bothering me and I felt Joan could be helpful with it, I had no qualms at the end of the day saying, 'Do you have a minute? I'd like to have a glass of wine and chat with you.' Linda Evans is also wonderful in that area. I felt we all responded to each other."

Kate O'Mara, a fellow British actress, also had a part in *Dynasty* for one season. She has only kind words for Collins. "I think she revels in the role," says O'Mara. "I'm convinced that's why she's so good at it. She's able to play Joan Collins off-screen as well. I mean I've never seen her looking less than absolutely wonderful. I don't know how she does it. I've learnt a few tricks from her, mind you."

Adds O'Mara, now back in England with her own touring company, "Joan is quite extraordinary and I admire her because she's a professional in her own way. And she keeps that sort of star image going the whole time, which is part of her charisma, part of her image. It's part of the reason that she's so enormously internationally popular because it (Hollywood) is a fantasy town. Joan is almost like the queen of the world and she gives people something to look at and admire—it's wonderful."

Indeed *Dynasty* and Joan have become internationally famous enough to lure former President Gerald Ford and his wife, Betty, as well as Henry Kissinger, to appear, albeit in walk-on parts, on the show. Hardly a week passes without Joan Collins getting at least a mention in a newspaper, a magazine, or a TV show. In both 1982 and 1983, she won the Golden Globe Award for "Best Actress in a TV Drama." At the ceremony the first year, Joan, ever gracious and also grateful, thanked the one person who might have come between her and Alexis: "I would like to thank Sophia Loren for turning down the part."

For Joan, *Dynasty* has spawned something of her own personal dynasty, including her own line of lingerie, hats, fake jewelry, blouses, and, for a time, a perfume, Scoundrel, in honor of Alexis. "Dynasty" clothes, as well, are now sold off the rack.

As a further measure of her celebrity value, she was also able to pull in a reported one hundred twenty-five thousand dollars for five hours in West

Germany. "First, she got $7,000 for a quickie TV appearance there," a magazine tabulated. "Then she pocketed a $26,000 pelt for taping a fur salon commercial. Then she got a diamond necklace worth about $12,000 for an appearance in a jewelry store and two free cars for appearing at a car dealership." Then, incredibly, in the last moments of her earning spree she won a cool seven thousand dollars in a lottery draw. Joan's circle of friends has also expanded, though not always, she points out, through her own design. "Woodwork friends," she quips. In view of her superstar status, the demands on her time are enormous. Her schedule is packed.

As Joan told one talk-show host in England, "A lot of people find it hard to keep up with me. People say some of my friends must be clones—there is one for the day shift and one for the night shift. I'm very lucky. I have a lot of joie de vivre and am able to do a lot of things." On the same show she also pointed out how in one month, "there weren't five days when I didn't go without getting on a plane. I was in London. Acapulco to Los Angeles to Barbados to Miami to Los Angeles to New York and then to Los Angeles again."

Despite the success that the show has brought her, ever since 1986 there have been reports that Joan Collins will leave the cast. As she told the *New York Post* then, "I'm going off; I'm going to produce my own movies." But, luckily for her audience, she added, "But I am allowed to change my mind."

Why is Joan's character Alexis, just like her sister Jackie's novels, such a worldwide phenomenon and why, too, is her role so crucial to the survival of this sensational soap opera? Marshall Fishwick, a professor of humanities and communications at Virginia Polytechnic, has looked into these questions. "I think *Dynasty* is a fascinating series at a fascinating time," he says. "Television has made classical revenge plots that have appeared in literature for the past two thousand years available to the masses at last." He continues, "Alexis is the character who frequently appears in Greek drama as the spoiler, the person who represents the dark side of the equation. She is the person who is constantly taunting the people who are working at the will of God. Therefore, she provides the tension in the show and allows it to continue after it would normally become sentimental and pedestrian. She always represents the unexpected and perhaps the deceptive side that we always try to hide." Alexis's personality, sometimes such an affront to viewers and their more civilized behavior, he says, reflects the change and confusion of society's values.

"I think she represents a reappraisal of the Western attitude that bigger is better and the good guys always win. After Vietnam and Watergate, we will never have the easy and simplistic view that we got from television comedies such as *I Love Lucy* or *Leave It to Beaver.*"

The professor also says Joan's exit from *Dynasty* would be highly detrimental to the series; in fact, he believes it would mean the end of the show. "It would be like replacing Jackie Gleason in *The Honeymooners*. She has become almost archetypal."

Already Joan Collins has been preserved in wax in Madame Tussaud's Museum in London. The decision to cast her, according to Juliet Simpkins, head of press and publicity there, was unanimous. "As the *Dynasty* series grew in popularity," she recalls, "we decided that it was absolutely essential to have her, an internationally known figure, in the museum. And our visitors enjoy glamour." The sculptor was Muriel Pearson. The sitting was done at Joan's home in California, where Pearson talked with her subject while getting precise measurements and photographs of her head and body from every possible angle.

The waxwork took slightly longer than the six months it usually takes to complete one. The reason was that Joan posed lying on a chaise longue instead of merely standing. Her gold-lamé dress, designed by *Dynasty*'s Nolan Miller, is slit to reveal just a little thigh. Copies of her diamond bracelet, ring, and earrings, and an emerald necklace decorate the upper part of her body. "There is something very solitary about posing for an artist," says Joan. "You turn off the phone and the television, and you sit by yourself. Everybody should try to take that space to clear their mind. I try to do it every day even on a train or bus."

Apparently there are few such moments in her life. In fact, the unveiling of the Joan Collins waxwork was held at Heathrow's Penta Hotel during a stopover Joan made in London one Saturday. This was the only time Joan, eager to see it, had available then. "Joan was utterly professional," says Simpkins. "She was very pleased. But we didn't quite get the hair right so Joan adjusted it." The waxwork of her dominates the museum's conservatory section. Reclining on a white wicker chaise longue, she occupies center stage in the company of, among other waxworks, J. R. Ewing (Larry Hagman), Agatha Christie, Liza Minnelli, Martina Navratilova, and even one of her sister Jackie's severest critics, author Barbara Cartland.

Though Jackie has yet to become a waxwork, she can take pleasure in knowing that she helped mold Joan into *Dynasty*'s Alexis with *The Stud* and *The Bitch*.

Private Lives . . . Jackie

Jackie Collins, it seems, has two distinct images. On the one hand, she is a housewife, homebody, and earth mother. On the other, as one talk-show host put it, "She has the image of a fierce tiger lady surrounded by publicity agents and Hollywood glitz." Admitting to the latter, Jackie says, "But only for two weeks a year when I do my book promotion tours. For the rest of the time I lead a perfectly normal life with my three wonderful kids."

So what is the private Jackie Collins like, after all. She lives in Beverly Hills, and she is a married woman. Nevertheless, Jackie states categorically that she is not a Hollywood wife. Indeed, by her own definition of that label, which she gave to *People* magazine in 1983, it would seem that she is telling the truth. "The Hollywood wife," she told them, "gets up in the morning, has her session with her exercise coach, has a massage, gets her nails fixed. Then she eats a lettuce leaf at Ma Maison, where she pays a fortune for it. She bitches to her lady friends that her husband is no longer sleeping with her but with someone else. Then she and her friends will set off for La Grande Shop where they will buy things they don't need, like a $3,000 fun fur. The Hollywood wife then goes home, yells at a Mexican maid, then says to her husband when he comes home from the studio exhausted, 'Now, we have a party tonight.' "

Jackie also pointed out, in that same article, other features of the Hollywood wife: "She has a look, usually created by a plastic surgeon, that defies any age category. The average wife is between 30 and 50. She fades away after that or her husband divorces her. Hollywood wives all look the same. They wear Maud Frizon shoes, Adolfo, Bill Blass or Oscar de la Renta designer ensembles. They carry Louis Vuitton bags. They go to Jessicas for their nails; José Elsters for their hair. They shop on Rodeo Drive at Gucci and Giorgio. They all know 'wonderful little dressmakers' and 'wonderful little caterers.' The chic thing is to have an exercise instructor come to the house.

"To live in this town," Jackie says, "you have to disregard totally all the Hollywood bullshit. You have to not want anything from anybody and not care what parties you're invited to." Then, almost tongue-in-cheek, Jackie adds, "There is nothing wrong with being a Hollywood wife—except they live in a vacuum. They actually say things like, 'I need a new dress,' and you say, 'But you spent $4,000 for a dress last week,' and they say, 'But I need it.' " Jackie gives an example of the insular, circumscribed existence of the xenophobic Hollywood wife by quoting a woman she knows: "Honey, my Rolls gets to the edge of Beverly Hills and automatically turns around and comes home."

Jackie's habits of living could not be more different than a Hollywood wife. "I don't spend my husband's money," she declares. "I spend my own. I don't worry what I'm going to wear to a party. I haven't worn a dress in years. A Hollywood wife would never be caught in my shoes. They cost about twenty-five dollars." Indeed, Jackie's lifestyle bares no resemblance to the description she gave magazines and newspapers of Hollywood wives while promoting her book of that title. But she has certainly come a long way from the days when she would cut off the bottoms of Joan's outfits to get even with her glamorous sister.

Nowadays, Jackie has a sumptuous mansion in the heart of Beverly Hills, complete with an outdoor swimming pool and, of course, a writer's den. It is the same den where she created *Hollywood Wives, Hollywood Husbands* and *Rock Star,* among some of her other best-sellers. As she told Britain's *Today* newspaper, "If you have a successful pattern, stick to it." The same applies to her interior design. Fake-fur scatter cushions reminiscent of seventies fashion decorate her floors. Indeed, Jackie seems to have a special affection for seventies styles. Even her taste in clothes—body-hugging Lycra, leopard skin—dates back to that period.

In a *New York Post* fashion spread on her, Jackie revealed, "I always travel first class, but skimp on other things." Itemizing her wardrobe, which appeared in accompanying photos, Jackie said her black tank top, for example, set her back a mere four dollars. "Classics are the only way to go if you travel a lot," Jackie advised. "My slacks ($100) are straight-legged which means they'll always be in style. I also used to travel with expensive jewelry, but I spent more time worrying about losing it or having to put it in a hotel safe. Now I just bring costume jewelry. But if I do bring any expensive piece, I wear it." In the luggage department, she had this to say: "Don't buy expensive luggage. It's sure to rip or get ripped off. I use plain black luggage with a lot of stickers all over it."

Unlike Joan, once spotted toting more than twenty pieces of luggage, Jackie travels light. "Beige shoes go with almost everything and that's it," Jackie says. "I don't believe in dresses. I pack black slacks. I bring four pairs: one silk, one leather, two gabardine for a week's tour. I would also pack four silk blouses, four T-shirts and a couple of jackets and mix 'n' match them." With her book tours packed with appearances, Jackie sticks to a system that avoids any last second slips-ups. "Make a list," she says. "This way you won't find you've left your belt or some other essential at home. I lay all my clothes flat in one suitcase, with tissue in between, so nothing wrinkles. In a second I pack shoes, bags, and roll my sweaters."

With all Jackie's millions, she does not have to dress to impress. Her home is equally unpretentious. Though on the outside it may look like one of the homes in *Dynasty,* inside it is homey and understated. In her pleasantly cluttered study both framed book jackets and hand-drawn birthday cards from her children hang on the walls. Her den looks more like a family gathering place than a writer's quarters. There is no typewriter. (She does not type.) There are no files or notebooks on display, either. There is a small, neat pine desk, family photos, and hundreds of soul and rock-and-roll tapes.

Jackie's manuscripts are hidden away in a corner cupboard. The only two people to see the pages before they are sent off to her publisher are husband Oscar and her secretary. There are few corrections or rewrites. It takes Jackie generally about a year to complete a novel. "I just write," she says. "I don't keep notes. I begin with a title. Then with a name. Distinctive names of characters are very important. I love it. I make up the story as I go along. Agony for me isn't in the writing, but in getting to the desk."

What of her output? Is the private Jackie Collins turned on by her own plots? Do the fantasies and adventures of her characters ever get translated into her own life?

"Well I don't rush off with an ax and kill someone after I've written a good violence scene," Jackie says. "And the sex scenes don't turn me on, because if they did I'd never get any work done. I wouldn't have the time. I read Harold Robbins to get turned on."

The designer-label possessions that seem to either cling to, drip from, or surround many of her characters are largely absent from Jackie's real-life environment. This holds true as well for the art on the walls of her home. The paintings are neither hugely expensive nor for show or investment purposes, but simply for her own pleasure. Art Deco is a style that she particularly likes.

Her collection of friends are not extensions of some of the hypersexed, self-indulged, excessively materialistic characters in her works. She does go to parties and mix with the stars, but most of this type of socializing is strictly research. "People treat me like the barman," she says. "You know, it's set 'em up, Jackie, and I'll tell you everything—you can talk about it, but don't mention any real-life names."

While many of her characters may bed-hop and visit their divorce lawyers and plastic surgeons all in the course of a chapter, Jackie has shared her life with the same man, Oscar Lerman (owner of the Tramp discos in London and Los Angeles), for over twenty years, and with her three children, Tracy, Tiffany, and Rory.

For Oscar's continuing support, Jackie vows that she will always be grateful. "He has always believed in me," she says. "When I first met my husband I hadn't finished my first book, *The World Is Full of Married Men*. I thought if I sent it around to publishers, I'd be putting myself up for rejection.

Right away, he kept insisting. 'You can do it.' I haven't forgotten that. My husband is incredibly supportive."

But Oscar does not play Svengali to Jackie. Of the balance of power in their marriage, she says, "He's in control of his life—not mine. We have an equal relationship. He doesn't tell me what to do, and I don't tell him. That's the secret of a good marriage."

Jackie believes strongly in marital fidelity, which in her view may be more difficult for men than women to achieve. However, she thinks that women should not rush into marriage without first enjoying life—and a man—for a time. "You should never get married," she cautions, "only to ask yourself, 'What have I missed?' "

Contrary to the impression left by her characters, who dabble in sex with people who may or may not belong to them, Jackie is something of a purist. "I don't see any point in getting married," she declares, "if you're not going to be faithful."

Jackie, however, can understand why certain women have affairs, though it would be unimaginable for her to do so. "I've been very lucky," she explains. "I'm never bored. But a lot of women don't have anything else in their lives. If you don't work and just go to the beauty salon to have your nails done and legs waxed, and your children are growing up and don't need you as much, I can understand that if an attractive man comes into your life and gives you the attention you're craving, it could be easy to have an affair. But to me there's something about the situation that's not true."

During an interview soon after the publication of *Rock Star,* Video Hits-1 veejay Bobby Rivers asked Jackie whom she would choose if she could make love to any rock star in the world. "I'm not really attracted to rock stars," Jackie answered. "But if I had to choose one it would be Elvis Presley when he was thin and gorgeous."

She attributes the success of her own marriage to several factors, not the least of which is, "We're truly best friends, and I enjoy talking to Oscar more than anyone I know." She adds: "Although we spend so much time together, we also leave each other alone enough so that we're not living in each other's pockets."

Whereas in the past it was usually the wife who relocated to accommodate a husband's job situation, in the Lerman family it was Jackie's idea to move from London to Los Angeles. And Oscar had no problem with this. That move, according to Jackie, would make all the difference in the world to her career. Out of that transatlantic crossing came the blockbuster, *Hollywood Wives*, and the rest is history. Jackie became a novelist with film-star status, something she believes would have never happened back in England. "America is the land of opportunity," she says, "and I think if the Americans like you, they *really* like you and take you to their heart. I've been really lucky in America. I think there's this kind of attitude in America where if you have a Ferrari, people come up to you and say, 'That's great, I want one.' But in England they might scrawl along the side, 'Rich scum.' There doesn't seem to be that attitude in England of, 'I can get it if I want it and I work hard enough.'"

The move also produced a whole new set of friends for the couple. "We're forever visiting them and discussing them with each other afterwards," Jackie says. "It's odd because I would have thought people would have backed away from me, but I have more friends than ever."

Her enormous financial success has not strained any friendships. "The toughest test of friendship or romance involves money," Jackie explains. "If you lend a friend money, and the debt isn't paid back in six months, the friend starts treating you badly. It's as if the unpaid debt is your fault. Money can come between people. It's divisive. People who don't have money resent people who do have money." But Jackie has a rather unique solution in this area: "I don't lend money anymore. If a friend says, 'I need $1,000 now,' I just give it as a gift." As for the distribution of money in her marriage, Jackie says, "I make more money now than my husband. I regard that money as mine. But I use it as ours. My husband is a secure man. He doesn't encroach on my career yet he is always looking after me. He watches my accountant. I feel this is *our* success."

Douglas Hayward, a friend from London who visits with them in Los Angeles, remarks, "Oscar is lovely, easygoing, and relaxed. He's a successful businessman. He's made it in his own right. He doesn't need to compete anymore."

Of the two sisters, Bob Tanner, today chairman and managing director of W. H. Allen, says, "Joan always left business to a husband, and she always had a different husband. Jackie's husband was a different kind of man and a constant man. I like Oscar." Of Jackie, he says, "I like her very much. She's good to work with. She's fussy about covers and very keen about her photographs, which she always supplied." In contrast to Joan, who always struck him as "a very nervous and uncertain person . . . she would eat very little and was always touching up her face in this vanity-box mirror," he remembers Jackie turning up at the White Elephant restaurant in a sweatshirt. What's more, contrary to the sisters' disclaimers, Tanner believes there is a hint of rivalry between the two. "Probably Joan saw the success of Jackie," he remarks, "and realized that she could not go on acting forever."

Just how much money has Jackie Collins reaped from her best-selling novels? In response to a question about her net worth, Jackie once told a journalist: "I think it's very tacky to discuss how much money one has. I will say that I have a lot, but further than that I will not go." At the same time she also said, "I love the money. I'm not knocking it, and I think it's sensational that so many people are buying my books, but I basically write to please myself."

Whatever the grand total, it probably would not alter her style of life all that much. Jackie remains, by all accounts, down-to-earth and empty of affectation. Though she has a cleaning woman three times a week at her home, Jackie still does the floors herself. She cooks all the family meals. "I'm eccentric by Hollywood standards," Jackie admits. "I answer my own door and telephone and drive a beat-up old Cadillac." Of course, Jackie reminds that even with these chores, she manages to write her best-selling novels. Nowadays she still keeps to the same schedule, up by 7 A.M. for family and housework, at her desk writing by 9 A.M. and laying down her pen by 6:30 P.M., as she did when starting out to become a published writer almost two decades ago. "If the phone rings," Jackie says, "it's usually a friend who can't wait to unload the latest scandalous tidbit."

Evenings are for family. Her three daughters have always been her priority above anything else. She says that she has a very close and loving relationship with them, and they are all fans of her books. "They started to read my books about four years ago," Jackie says of her children, all of them now young ladies, and then, mischievously, she continues, "And knowing which side their bread is buttered on, they absolutely love them." Away from the book-promotion circuit, Jackie Collins is best and most familiarly known as, simply, Jackie Lerman. The Lerman household also has two friendly yellow Labrador dogs. One visitor, Joan, is not crazy about them jumping on her.

To Tracy, Tiffany, and Rory, Jackie Collins remains just plain Mum. "They won't even watch me on the television anymore," she says. "I'm just Mum, you know." Then, proudly, Mum adds, "They're smashing people to be around." Said Jackie's late father: "Like that of her own mother, Elsa, Jackie's first priority is the welfare of her husband and children. She is a most protective mother. I cannot reconcile her own life-style with that portrayed in her books." Admiring, as well, of his son-in-law Oscar's longevity in the usually short-lived disco business, Joe Collins said of him, "Oscar has fitted into our family life very well. He and my son Bill, who have been business partners in a car-hire firm and also in an art gallery, are particularly good friends." Once Bill was a deejay in Oscar's club. And Jackie dedicated *Rock Star*, "For my brother, Bill Collins, who has always been there for me."

"Jackie has chosen a role with husband and children," says friend Douglas Hayward, "and she doesn't like traveling outside the circle. She seeks comfort in family and a few close friends." When Jackie and Oscar venture out it is usually to a Hollywood party where, says Jackie, she never comes up short of themes. "All I have to do is just sit and talk to someone," she says, "and an idea for a new novel comes to me immediately." Jackie's other favorite observatories include two fashionable restaurants, Spago and Le Dome. "When Jackie walks in somewhere," says Hayward, "she always has a strong presence."

Hayward says further: "Both Jackie and Joan are very strong characters. They're not women who hang around and giggle a lot. Joan can be frivolous and light and funny, but underneath there's a very strong personality. They both have a great sense of humor and incredible loyalty. They're both very worldly. They're instinctive. There's no one academic or intellectual that would frighten them. They hold their own. Jackie handles interviewers incredibly well—she takes the mickey out of them before they can do it to her. They adore each other but there is a great rivalry which I think is quite healthy. Joan is more outgoing than Jackie."

Much as Jackie likes the California sun, the atmosphere does not always suit her. "What's the point of getting all dressed up to sit in a dark movie theater for two hours for a film premiere," Jackie wonders aloud. She prefers to stay home and read, but when Joan is in town, she says, "There are three parties in an evening, and Joan says, 'First we'll go here and then here and then here . . .' "

The chauvinistic attitude of some locals also irks Jackie. "Being a good-looking woman in Hollywood is difficult," she notes. "Men are scared off by beautiful, talented women. They feel threatened that a woman could do their job better."

In a 1984 *People* magazine interview, Joan said of Jackie: "I think Jackie felt for a time that men are takers and women are used. I don't feel that way. I feel that sexual relationships are equal, and that women are entitled to have as free a sex life as men." Jackie remarked then, "I don't believe in a double standard. I think there should be a better balance between the sexes and maybe in my own teeny way, I might help."

Though the sisters may not agree on every issue, they are, despite rumors to the contrary, the best of friends. "My sister and I get along very well," says

Jackie. "She reads my books, and I watch *Dynasty*. I enjoy having my name known, but I don't have all the burdens of being a movie or TV star—or rock star. People know your name, but not always your face. I do get recognized, but there's always that book between the person and me."

A chief regret of both is that their mother is not alive to see and share in their successes. Jackie champions Joan for making women over forty fashionable. "Women seem to get better and better," Jackie says. "They're not so hung up on being twenty-two forever. I never want a face-lift. Imagine, going to a hospital voluntarily to get cut up for no reason." Probably there would be no reason for either Jackie or Joan to sign up. After all, the two sisters love their lines, whether written (Jackie) or acted (Joan).

Private Lives . . .
Joan

Offstage, Joan has yet to achieve the marital stability that gives so much comfort to Jackie in her life. To date, Joan has four ex-husbands. By the time Oscar and Jackie married, in 1966, Joan's second marriage, to Anthony Newley, was starting to fall apart after four years. Nevertheless, the Lerman wedding was held at the Newleys' home in Beverly Hills. Joan remembers, "As I stood behind Jackie, I realized that nobody had ever really loved me."

Certainly Joan's first husband, the actor Maxwell Reed, had not shown her even the slightest kindness even before their nuptials. Asked why she married him, Joan told *US* magazine in 1985: "I haven't really analyzed it enough, I suppose. I think I was proving that I was worthwhile after this man had raped me, that I could make him love me. And after all, he wasn't just some, you know, shlep. He was extremely handsome, and he had been my favorite movie star when I was a girl at school." The marriage lasted under a year. The divorce would be one of the first times a woman was ever sued for alimony. "He sued me with the excuse he *made* my career," she sniffs. "Pretty pathetic."

But even that dreadful experience did not cause Joan to swear off marriage, something that would

create as much havoc in her life as it made for
peace in Jackie's. In part, the fact that Joan could
empty her mind of Reed is indicative of her capac-
ity to deal with anger. No collector of injustices is
Joan. "I have the attitude that if something makes
you upset," she says, "then you better get angry
about it quickly, then forget all about it. Sitting
around brooding won't do a damn bit of good."
Her technique has worked so effectively that more
than thirty years later she almost failed to notice
that the lawyer, Marvin Mitchelson, who repre-
sented her in her fourth divorce, was the same person who, as a young man, had served her on a
movie set with the Reed divorce papers. Further,
her fourth husband, like the first, would also ask
for alimony.

Her second marriage, to Anthony Newley, would
last seven years and produce two children, Tara
Cynara and Alexander Anthony ("Sacha"). By then,
1963, Joan had some experience, a few affairs, behind her. She was thirty. Remarkably, with all the
hard work she had done in Hollywood, Joan had
nothing to show for it. If she was able to acquire
roles, boyfriends, and now a second husband, certainly the same could not be said of material possessions. She owned nothing, not a house nor any
art to speak of. It had never been her intention to
wait for a husband to provide them; instead, she
had a carefree attitude about such things. It was
just too boring to think about saving money.

Still, it was a wonderful time for Joan when the
couple moved into what she would remember as
her first real home as an adult. Until then, Harley
House, where she spent her early years, still
seemed like home to her. For brief periods between films, romances, or husbands, she would return to the nest. The house that Joan and Tony
settled on was an Edwardian mansion, named Fri-

ar's Mead, in London. Joan, now with infant children and her career somewhat stagnant, devoted
herself to making the house elegant and beautiful.
To this end she hired the noted interior designer
Robin Guild. No sooner had the work been com-
pleted and the Newley family really settled in,
however, than Joan would be uprooted again, this
time briefly to New York and then Hollywood. The
reason was Tony's career. Just as he was moving
ahead, it seemed to Joan that she was going nowhere. Remembering her previous migrations on
Warren Beatty's behalf, Joan described herself as
"a camp follower."

Tony was, by her account, a workaholic who
made no secret of his affairs with other women.
The end of their seven-year marriage was virtually
spelled out in an erotic musical comedy, *Can Hieronymous Merkin Ever Forget Mercy Humppe and
Find True Happiness?*, written and directed by
Newley, who also starred in it. He unveiled his
longings for another woman in the play. To Joan,
who did not even get the part she wanted, the show
was a heartache.

Joan was rejected for the lead comedienne role
she hoped might lift her career out of the doldrums, and only got to play a smaller role because
she would be there with her family anyway. Joan
brought her two children on location to London
and Malta for five months. With the final break in
the marriage, Joan, despite her costly first divorce,
sought only child support, no alimony. "As long as
the children were taken care of," she reflected
later, "I figured that I would be able to continue
working."

Though Joan frequently tends to downplay her
maternal skills, by all accounts she is an uncom-
monly good mother. "I suppose I could be called
an unnatural mother," she says, "because I don't

really enjoy cooking, cleaning, and getting up to make breakfast. But I love spending time with my children. They're bright and funny."

Joan's autobiography describes a difficult period in 1965 when she was caring for her two infants— both under two years old—and became ill with what her doctor called "puerperal fever." Twenty-two-month-old Tara, wildly jealous of the attention that might be taken away from her and lavished on her baby brother, refused to leave her mother's side. Since Sacha got to sleep in a crib in his parents' bedroom, Tara wanted to sleep in the room, too. While Joan was lifting or holding her newborn son, her baby daughter was pulling at her arms and jumping into her lap as well. Tara had become all too accustomed to her mother's total devotion. Joan had taken her infant daughter everywhere, even on location. Tara was not about to surrender all this attention to a baby brother. Often, while this sibling rivalry was being played out in its most primitive and exacting form, Tony was away at the theater. And the German nanny seemed to be deaf to the wailings of Tara and Sacha in the middle of the night. Thus Joan awoke one morning to find herself feeling like death. Her doctor diagnosed her condition as "puerperal fever," a condition resulting from infection of the placental site. The doctor gave Joan what she called a "wonder drug" and advised Joan to take a break from her duties as a mother to get back her strength. Joan, according to a Portuguese housekeeper who later worked for Joan and Newley, is a superb mother. "Joan is one of the best mothers who is an actress," says the housekeeper, Alice Ferreira. "If she was home, she liked to bathe and tuck her children into bed. She always tried to take them with her when she went on location."

At one point Joan and Tony brought the housekeeper's ten-year-old son to Beverly Hills from Lisbon, Portugal, where he was living with his grandmother. "I was very ill with the Hong Kong flu," the housekeeper remembers. "Joan not only cooked for her own children but mine as well."

Ferreira remembers her years with the Newleys on Summit Drive in Beverly Hills with great affection. Her husband worked for the Newleys as well, as a chauffeur, though "Joan liked to drive herself." The large eight-bedroom house was white with a green front door. "At the time, green was Joan's favorite color," the housekeeper remembers. "Though she also liked peach." The house was always filled with fresh, cut flowers. Joan's favorite: lilies of the valley. Joan's bedroom was done in green and white, and the living room in yellow. There was a swimming pool outside, and when Joan was home she would use it.

Ferreira came there originally as a cook, but because of her affection for children, Joan entrusted her with their care when she was away. After the Newleys' divorce, it would be Ferreira who brought the children back to London for Christmas and other holidays. Joan was re-married to Kass and living there, and Tony was still in Beverly Hills. "Joan treated me like family," she says. "She was very generous. She gave me a lot of presents. Her clothes, a necklace, a leather handbag. I ate the same things as them."

Though Joan, she says, likes caviar and champagne best of all, there were also times that she would try Portuguese dishes. Casual dinners were usually things like chicken, roast beef, and duck. At least twice a week there would be six to eight guests for dinner, she says, and Jackie and her husband Oscar were frequently among them. There were also big parties with many different dishes either catered or cooked by the housekeeper. One party Ferreira remembers was a sit-down dinner for ballet stars Rudolph Nureyev and Margot Fontaine with, among others in attendance, Frank Sinatra and his then-wife Mia Farrow.

Most every day, the housekeeper remembers, Jackie would come by for tea with Joan. "They were so close and good to each other," she remembers. "They'd just sit around and laugh together or talk about the children." Frequently the sisters, she says, went shopping together. "Jackie is a big girl and Joan is more petite," she says, "but there's no real difference between them. They're both two very glamorous, happy sisters." Frequently the Newley and Lerman clans would all get together for afternoons by the pool at either of their homes. Joan, the housekeeper recalls, liked to do her own marketing, but while out of town left her the credit cards to do the shopping. "She never got mad with me," Ferreira reports. "If something bothered her, she would tell you exactly what she felt, and that was it."

Around the house, according to Ferreira, Joan often dressed casually, in jeans and without any makeup on. She also regards Joan as "a very truthful person" with all her friends. "Joan used to talk on the phone a lot," she reports further, "and she always took her calls." She was also generous with advice and, according to the housekeeper, Jackie also came by to seek it. "I think Jackie looked up to Joan," she remembers. "When she was upset about something, she would come over to talk to Joan."

No matter how many dinners or parties or telephone calls Joan had, in the opinion of the housekeeper, she always put the children first. Joan set rules, too. "She was very strict about report cards," the housekeeper says. "And she made the children do their homework and have dinner before they were allowed to watch TV for a half hour each night. Bedtime was seven o'clock.

"I'd go back to work for Joan in a minute," says the housekeeper who saw her and the children about four years ago. "Joan Collins is a beautiful human being. She is nothing like Alexis." Of Joan's two children by Newley, she says the oldest, Tara, is more like her mother; and the son, Sacha, like his father. "Tara is very quick, very bright, and very beautiful," Ferreira says. "Sacha is very quiet, intelligent, and likes to write." Currently, both of them, in their twenties, live in Europe. Joan visits them every few weeks.

"I really hated it when Joan and Tony got divorced," the former housekeeper remembers. "I always thought they should be together." She adds: "I think Joan needs somebody in her life. It should be somebody with a strong personality who tells her what to do because Mr. Kass (Joan's next husband) was demanding and they had a great love at first. Maybe Tony is too sweet and soft."

Joan's late father liked Kass best of all the husbands. He detested Reed completely. "Tony Newley, I didn't think, was a good marriage for her," Joe Collins also said, "but it was good because it gave her two lovely children."

Douglas Hayward, tailor to both Newley and Kass, was with them the night Joan met Kass, and has a different view of things. "It's difficult to see Joan in terms of a match," he allows. "But I think probably Tony was the best because he had his own strength. He had a very strong character that stood up against hers but did not challenge her in her own area. It was a balance of two equal strengths, which worked. Joan's strength is such that she makes people—not intentionally though—give way to her."

Newley, since remarried, has also preserved his

dignity in the face of Joan's tell-all autobiography. Though stung by her descriptions, he reportedly turned down a mega-advance for his own autobiography. He made his opinion of Joan's autobiography plain when he told *People* magazine, "To the great unwashed public the woman is a star. But to those who know her, she's a commodity that would sell her bowel movement."

After they parted ways in 1970, Joan moved back to London where she resumed working again. It was then that she became seriously involved with Ron Kass, an American record company executive based there. "He was the first man I had ever met," she once said, "who thought of me first and himself second." They married in 1972. Their union would produce a third child, Katyana Kennedy (Katy), with whom Joan would prove to be an almost superhuman mother. The first five years, by Joan's account, were the happiest in her adult life. "Everything was the way you always wanted it to be," she told *Parade* magazine. "Ron and I were extremely happy. He had a good job. I was working in English films and television, the two children had adjusted to going to school and the baby was great. It was just sort of perfect."

At the outset of their marriage, Kass rescued Joan from the horror film genre by optioning one of her favorite Noel Coward plays, *Fallen Angels*. He produced it, and Joan was teamed up with Susannah York to play two acerbic-tongued ladies drooling over a Frenchman. Kass would also be one of the coproducers of *The Stud* and *The Bitch*. Later he engineered her first huge contract with Revlon and he also negotiated her *Playboy* deal.

That happiness would not last. Five years later, in 1975, when they moved back to Los Angeles, Kass lost his job and Joan found she was again an unknown. Money became a big problem. Joan

scraped up whatever work she could—foreign celluloid films and TV bit parts—just to stay afloat.
She tried Actualization—est with bathroom privi-
leges—workshops where she was urged to be patient with Kass until he could recover his self-
worth after the shock of the job loss.

Even their return two years later, in 1977, to
London, could not repair the relationship. In the
years after their divorce Kass would take credit for
getting Joan's career back on track. At the same
time, had Joan listened to him, she might well have
lost out on *Dynasty.* In a sense, Kass's role became
more a matter of investing his somewhat demolished ego in Joan instead of taking a chance on
himself again.

As Hayward explains: "Ron was a very tall good-
looking and lively man when they met. Joan and
Tony were just about finished. Kass was a nice
man, a good man, and in his way quite talented. He
was an efficient man. In the sixties music was ex-
ploding and he should have been the top man because he knew more than anyone. He had even
played the trombone and had degrees in law and
accountancy. But he was always a company man,
not an entrepreneur. He carried this over to Joan—
she was the strong boss. I think there was a strong
self-destruct in Ron."

The editor of the *Joan Collins Beauty Book,* Michael Alcock, remembers his editorial meetings
over four months, once every other week, with
Joan at her Mayfair (London) home. "Ron Kass
tried to be her business manager," Alcock remembers. "And she didn't like him being this. He was a
bit of a bumbler. Joan was short with him. 'Thank
you,' she would say, 'but we're not doing that.' Joan
had everything mapped out. He wanted to be involved, but a man can't write a woman's beauty

book. He was better at looking over her royalty statements."

To the late Joe Collins's thinking, "Joan never seemed to find a man who was her match. She always had more strength, more resilience, than any of the husbands she chose."

What would test Joan's strength more than any other event in her life was the almost-fatal injury of her youngest daughter, Katy, then eight, in August of 1980. She was hit by a car and arrived comatose at a hospital. That near-tragedy would be the only reason as well that Joan stayed with Kass as long as she did—eleven years in total. By then their marriage had deteriorated to a point where the only solution was divorce.

Doctors held out little hope that Katy would make it through the night, and even if she did, she would likely suffer permanent brain damage. Determined to prove them wrong, Joan and Ron managed to breathe life back into their beloved daughter Katy by talking to her and comforting her for hours on end.

Katy had been hit by a car as she stepped out onto what she had thought was a country lane, and thrown against a concrete curb. At the time Katy was with her best friend—at whose house in Ascot, an area about an hour by car from London and famous for its prestigious racetrack, she was staying while her own parents were away in Paris on business. Apparently Katy and her friend, who escaped uninjured, had been pretending to chase a boy who had teased them, and they rushed onto the road through a garden gate. The nanny, according to Joan, had been distracted from watching the two girls at that instant.

The car that hit Katy was driven by an eighteen-year-old youth, ironically named Collins. The young man had been driving his father back from a medical examination.

Katy was taken by ambulance to a local hospital, where doctors pronounced her case hopeless. It was agreed that it would be advisable, risky as it was, to move Katy (who was comatose) to the more sophisticated Central Middlesex hospital in Acton, a suburb of London. Europe's most eminent brain surgeon was associated with Central Middlesex. It was to Central Middlesex that Joan, Ron, and Tara, Katy's older stepsister, rushed when they heard the news. They had learned of the accident in their hotel at two in the morning of Saturday, August 2—and only three and a half hours later, thanks to a friend's private plane, had left Paris for London.

They rented a trailer and lived for the next six weeks in the parking lot of the hospital. They spent almost every waking hour by Katy's bedside. After eight days in a coma, Katy finally opened her eyes. Six weeks later, though still unable to speak or walk, Katy was taken home by her parents.

Joan remembers those harrowing first moments seeing Katy in a coma. "I think I was sort of driven by an atavistic, maternal ferocity," she says. "I didn't consciously think of anything other than the fact that, to make her survive, I had to pour my energy and joie de vivre and belief that she *was* going to survive into her."

Pat Hannam, a pediatric nurse, was then clerical officer of the unit where Katy was eventually moved from intensive care. Her job was taking care of mothers of patients as much as the sick children. "In all my years of nursing," Hannam, winner of a 1987 British Empire Medal for a lifetime of work with children, says, "I have never seen a more loving relationship between a mother and daughter. Joan would stroke Katy's face and hold her hand. There was so much contact and so much love. Joan did not want to leave Katy's bedside even to get something to eat. She felt she had to be Katy's strength. She willed her to get better. You *can* talk a child out of a coma. Doctors can only do so much. But the way Joan was there, she made Katy well with all her love and feeling."

After a few weeks, Hannam remembers, she says she urged Joan to rest and get some sleep. But Joan kept her vigil by Katy's bed. Though there was a shower in the trailer, frequently Joan would wash in the nurses' station in order to be near Katy every second, and also to avoid the crush of reporters in the parking lot. Even the lack of sleep and proper meals, according to Hannam, did not erode Joan's energy or spirit. "She never broke down," the nurse remembers. "There was never any hysteria."

Joan would have no part of any hopeless prognosis by some doctors, nor tears from friends and family who came to visit. "I had to protect Katy from any negative thoughts," she remembers. "I would just fight like a tiger about that. And when any of my family or friends came in and started to cry, I wouldn't allow it."

What particularly struck Nurse Hannam about Joan was that she never demanded special treatment. "Usually when stars come in," she says, "they make sure everybody knows within minutes who they are. With Joan it was never 'I'm a star and I want this,' only 'I'm Katy's mom.' In the unit where Katy was there were thirty-two beds divided into clusters of six. Masses of flowers and cards came for Katy, and Joan shared them with all the children. "It was never, 'Pin this card right here,'" Hannam remembers, "but Joan spreading the cards along all the shelves in the ward. She talked with their parents and introduced herself as Mrs. Kass."

A domestic worker who saw Joan the morning after the accident says that she had no idea then that she was a star. Though Joan always looked well-groomed, in slacks and blouses, she struck Maisie Johnson, mopping the floors in intensive care, as just an ordinary mother. "She didn't stop talking to her daughter for one minute," Johnson remembers. "She would even say, 'Katy, there's this lady cleaning the floor to make it nice for you.'"

Once Katy became more alert, Nurse Hannam recalls, Joan would sing to her. "Joan would do Katy's favorite nursery rhymes," she says, "and tell her, 'Katy, this is like it was when you were a little girl.'" Later Joan would wait for the therapist to come by to find out how to help Katy with the exercises she needed to do. Throughout the ordeal, Joan also showed a religious side to her personality. "Whenever a minister, rabbi, or priest would come to visit," the nurse says, "Joan and her husband would kneel down with them properly, with full respect."

Nurse Hannam says that she will never forget Katy's mom. Her husband, a lorry driver, also met Joan. The Hannams are also "pearlies," English people who work for charity in their communities. "Being true East Enders," says Hannam, "we appreciated Joan's down-to-earth and natural ways. I would go to task for her if she ever needed anything."

As a recipient of Joan's gratitude, Hannam received flowers, chocolate, and also bath oils from Fortnum and Mason's, one of the finest stores in the world. Her husband got a huge bottle of Cinzano in a velvet case, with a glass to go with it. Later on, Joan would bestow a gift of a machine to the neurosurgery department at London's Charing Cross Hospital for the opening of a new wing.

The road to Katy's full recovery would be long
and arduous. But Joan would be there every step of
the way. Asked by *Parade* in 1985 how she had
been able to find such strength inside herself, Joan
said, "Me? I faint when somebody tries to give me
an injection! And to see one's child in intensive
care, strapped up to every possible needle and IV
and blood transfusion—yeah, I *was* surprised. But
it made me realize afterward that I was really a
much stronger person than I'd thought. I also got
the feeling, very strongly, that if you believe in
something, it will happen. And I really believe
that."

Once Katy improved significantly, Joan was
back at work, largely in theater. Prior to the accident, Joan's two older children, Tara and Sacha,
were back living with them in London. Finding
that she and Kass were in more serious debt than
she realized, Joan attempted to sell the Beverly
Hills home that they had left behind. A close
friend, a devout Catholic, pleaded with Joan to stay
with Ron as a sign of "God's love for Katy."

The *Dynasty* offer would ultimately spell the end
of their marriage. Kass, fearing that they might be
sued for breach of contract, tried to hold Joan to a
deal they had with Triumph Productions for Joan
to do some plays. *Dynasty* not only conflicted with
her theater schedule, but also offered no definite
long-term commitment. Having effected Katy's recovery, Joan now believed that she herself was also
a survivor: "It's why I've felt that my career was
going to go on in some way or another. It doesn't
just happen. I wanted to become successful in Hollywood. And when the chance came, I worked at it,
deliberately worked at it. And not only in front of
the camera. I worked to become known. I must
have done one hundred fifty interviews in the first
year of *Dynasty.*" Part of her decision had to do

with Katy, still in physical therapy, benefiting from the outdoor life in California, where the warm weather was far more salutary than London's drizzle.

This time Joan went alone. Her marriages never did travel well. While working in *Dynasty,* Joan hired a woman to look after Katy. In 1983, Joan, by then a superstar, got legally unhitched from Kass. It was a bitter divorce in which Kass suggested that Joan was quite like Alexis in real life. According to a close friend of Joan's, however, Joan "stayed longer than most other people would." Three years later in 1986, Kass died of cancer, and Joan, the mother of his daughter, went to the funeral.

Joan remembers one of the astrologers, whom she has consulted over the years, telling her back in 1977, "You have the potential for incredible fame and success if you just apply yourself completely to what you're doing and don't allow yourself to get sidetracked."

Discipline characterizes Joan's life. Just as sister Jackie sticks to a writing schedule, Joan maintains a strict health regimen. "One's body is a machine," she says, "and you have to take care of it as much as any machine." Though she finds exercise a crashing bore, she uses a Universal body exerciser, a dynamic-tension form of exercise, on which she does her stretching and push-ups daily. Salads, chicken, and pasta are staples of her diet, and she also puts away a can of sardines a week. "I truly believe you are what you eat," she told *People* in 1983. "I basically eat anything I want, but not too much of it. I don't believe women should eat too much red meat and eggs." Joan, at five feet six inches and one hundred twenty pounds, avoids chocolate much as she loves it, and she hardly ever has dessert. At last published count *(People,* 1979), her measurements were 38-24-37.

"I have never missed a day of work because of illness," says Joan, who chases an infrequent cigarette with vitamins A and C "which I gobble up like candy." She abhors drugs. "They are the most destructive thing," she declares, "and I'm including sleeping pills and pep pills."

As a woman gets older, Joan cautions, she must take more care of herself. The *Playboy* pictures she did were intended to upgrade the image of women over forty. "I feel like I'll look pretty good when I'm old," she says. "But maybe then I won't care. I do know I don't want to be a sixty-year-old woman trying to look thirty-five."

In the looks department, the woman Joan most admires is also over forty, Farrah Fawcett. "Farrah is the only girl that I've ever looked at and found to be totally perfect," Joan admits. "Her hair, her skin, her body, her teeth, are all perfect." She adds: "I don't know quite about the brain—I haven't analyzed it."

As a measure of Joan's own brain power, she manages to juggle several tasks, all of them mentally demanding, at the same time. While being fitted or made up for a *Dynasty* scene, she may scribble notes for her novel. Not to mention, of course, that Joan has the responsibilities of a single parent, looking after Katy and hopping flights regularly to see her two older children. Over the last fourteen years Joan has also been a foster mother to an Indian girl, Fathimary Pragasm, whom she found through a foster parent program. Fathimary is now nineteen (as of 1989). Joan met her for the first and only time six years ago, in 1983, during the filming of TV program *This Is Your Life, Joan Collins,* in England. Fathimary was flown in as part of the show. Of their meeting, Joan told *US* magazine in 1985: "Well, I didn't speak a word of Hindi, and she didn't speak a word of English. But it was really sweet because she didn't know I was an actress; I'd written and told her I was a businesswoman. She was rather stunned—I don't think they have *Dynasty* in those parts of the Third World." Joan and Fathimary continue as pen pals, and Joan sends money.

Though disappointed by marriage, Joan remains a romantic. "Unfortunately, something seems to happen in marriages that go on for a long time," she says. "Something dies a bit or a lot." She makes a clear distinction between love and "in love." "Love is something you have for a child or grandmother," she explains. "In love has a lot to do with sex." Joan recommends sex highly though she also thinks of herself as something of a prude. "Sex is terribly good for you," she states. "If I'm in love with someone it's fantastic."

Of her attraction in more recent years to younger men, including the late actor, Jon-Erik Hexum, with whom she costarred in *The Making of a Male Model,* Joan told *US:* "Younger men, I think, accept strong women so much more. When I say younger men, I mean sort of forty. Over forty and they're a different generation. Women have changed so much in the last twenty, even ten, years. A strong, confident, beautiful woman is a terrible threat to many men—particularly if she's in a position of power. Because they will do anything to demean her. That attitude has gone down through history. With the exception of a few incredible women like Coco Chanel, Catherine the Great, the Duchess of Windsor, strong women were called unnatural." In sharp contrast to her image as the *Dynasty* vixen, Joan adds emphatically, "I like women a lot. I mean, I've got a lot of really good women friends."

Her best friend for life is Jackie. They are fiercely loyal to each other. Neither will tolerate any criticism of the other by outsiders. "I don't trade off her name," Jackie stresses, "and she doesn't trade off mine. You will never find one of us bringing up the other unless someone else does so first. And, then, it had better be positive, too."

Says Joan: "I believe very much in positive thinking. No one gives you the confidence or belief in yourself except yourself, and if you don't believe in this, it will show through."

Though yet to find her ideal husband, Joan also believes strongly in the power of love. And what, exactly, does love mean to this English ambassador of amour? "Really loving," says Joan Collins, "is caring about someone's welfare more than your own."

Their Father's Daughters

One of the most challenging roles in the lives of these Hollywood sisters was that of being their father's daughters. Until his death at eighty-six, in April 1988, Joe Collins was an enduring and powerful presence in both their lives. Cranky and critical as he sometimes sounded in his pronouncements about them, he would never be guilty of indifference in his lifetime.

Whether it was details of their births, teenage romances, marriages, careers, finances, or fame, Joe Collins had, it seemed, the last word. But, always, he was even-handed in his opinions. "I don't watch Joan on *Dynasty*," he told several interviewers. "It bores me to death." As for Jackie's books: "I read the first couple of pages and I think, 'Oh, Jackie, this is horrible language.' The sex I don't mind. It's the language, the four-letter words."

Yet there sometimes seemed to be a competitive edge to his remarks. Perhaps it had to do largely with the fact that Joe Collins himself had spent his life in show business as a theatrical entrepreneur. "Not so many years ago it was I who was the best-known member of our family," he wrote in his autobiography. "A top theatrical agent and entrepreneur. But today when I am out and about, people point to me and say, 'You know who that is, don't you? That's Joan and Jackie's father.' . . . I chuckle 'Real fame at last!' But personal fame was never my aim. I have been content to be 'Mr. Ten Per Cent.' "

The title of his autobiography, *A Touch Of Collins,* something of a play on the phrase "a touch of class," was largely an ode to himself. Understandably, he was enormously proud of Jackie and Joan, but he was quick to document every detail of his family heritage and his own achievements. If, for example, he mentioned the *Playboy* story on Joan, it would only be a reference point for stating how he staged the first nude revue in England before it was fashionable.

Joe Collins was always of prime importance to his dutiful daughters. But no matter what his instructions, whether it was telling Jackie which books not to read or advising Joan to avoid an acting career, they, like most youngsters, followed their own dreams. As Joe Collins put it: "My two eldest girls, Joan and Jackie, did not reach the top of their competitive fields on a plane of tranquility."

In later years, Joan would come to realize her father was often right in his thinking. Collins adamantly opposed Joan's first marriage to Maxwell Reed, a mistake that would take her over twenty years to admit to her father. At the most crucial moment in her career, Joan also sought his advice. Not since finding Joan her first agent when she was only sixteen had Joe been directly involved in her professional life. She arrived at his home in something of a panic about what to do about her *Dynasty* offer in view of the prior theater contract. Joe Collins ordered her to do *Dynasty*. This time she listened.

Joan saw more of her father in later years than Jackie did. In part, it was probably because her life, with all the divorces, was more unsettled. And

Joan was in London more frequently than Jackie, who would spend time with her father while on book tours there. On the flyleaf of *The Love Killers (Lovehead)*, Jackie wrote this inscription to him: "I know you won't read this one, but it is a good book." With *Hollywood Wives*, Jackie would inscribe it to both her father and his second wife: "To Irene and Daddy . . . Irene, for goodness sake, don't let him read this." Frequently during the early days of Jackie's marriage, Joe would turn up at Tramp to join her and Oscar. "Daddy, daddy," he remembered Jackie squealing happily as soon as she saw him.

"I am not put out when I see Joan on television in bed with some actor," he once explained. "So why don't I follow Jackie's work, too? An author creates a more personal relationship with the reader than an entertainer creates with an individual person in the audience. I feel it distasteful for a father to read his daughter's descriptions of sex."

Joe Collins, a proud man, would give this standard reply to people slyly inquiring about Joan's autobiography, *Past Imperfect*, in which she had been somewhat hard on him: "Haven't got around to reading it yet." He never would, either, saying, "That book is not relevant to my love for my daughter, or her love for me."

Joan, according to her father, later explained in a note that she had actually written the book with love, but in sorting out how she really felt in the most honest way about men, conveyed another impression. "And after all," she wrote to him, "you were the first man in my life." Later on, Joan would also tell him she regretted writing the book in the first place.

Yet some of the criticisms Joan wrote about her father, largely about his chauvinistic ways, he already knew about himself. Joe Collins, just like his daughters, would grow and change throughout his life. His second wife, Irene, herself a successful theatrical agent, would give him another shot at fatherhood. They had a daughter, Natasha, when Joe was sixty-five. And he would be far less critical and tyrannical with her than he had been with Joan and Jackie. The Hollywood Sisters could not believe, for example, that he let Natasha wear makeup when she was only sixteen since he had hollered at them for doing the same at that age. Ironically, Natasha, although brought up with more freedom than Joan and Jackie, would end up joining the British Army.

As a measure of the deep bond they felt with their father, even as adults they were not initially thrilled about his remarrying. In fact, Joe Collins did not tell them until after the ceremony. Joe's second wife, Irene, was thirty-three years younger than he, and what's more, three years younger than Joan and only five older than Jackie.

"I don't think the girls were at all happy to hear I had got married," Collins recalled. "Their reaction was instinctive: they were close to their late mother, and they thought it was wrong I should love anyone else." His new bride, Irene, had arrived in England from Germany on the day Elsa Collins died. Joe would meet her sometime later in the course of business. They married in 1967, five years after the death of Elsa.

Eventually, Joan and Jackie did come around. Jackie, according to her father, was the spokesperson, declaring, "We all think Irene is a fabulous person." Joan later told them to have a baby: and Jackie, whose second daughter was a year old, gave Irene her maternity outfits and baby clothes.

But Joe Collins would never countenance Joan's fourth husband, Peter Holm. "Joan and I are very close and I don't want to upset her in any way," he told one journalist. "She's made her bed and she's got to sleep in it." Joe Collins's eighty-third birthday would be the only one that Joan missed in his lifetime. He worried that something might be wrong with her. He found out two days later when Joan rang him from the *Dynasty* set telling him about everything except her marriage to Peter Holm. He heard about it when reporters started ringing him for his reaction.

Joe Collins had a full life. He loved his children and grandchildren, and they loved him, too. When he was laid to rest in April 1988 he knew at least that Jackie was well looked after by Oscar, whom he adored, and Joan was well rid of the man he could not stand, Peter Holm.

Peter Holm

It was in 1983 that Joan Collins met the man who would become her fourth husband, Peter Holm. The setting was a friend's house in London where she was posing for some photographs for a Spanish magazine. Peter was their next-door neighbor. They were introduced. Peter said very little. But apparently he made some kind of an impression on Joan because the next day, after a friend had to bow out of the premiere of *Superman III* at the last moment, Joan decided to ask Peter along as her escort. He readily agreed. "We got along famously," Joan told *US* magazine in 1985. "I said, 'If you're ever in L.A., look me up.' And he's very polite. Swedish polite. He kissed my hand at the door, said good night, and a week later, he called me and said he might be coming out to L.A. We've hardly been apart since then."

It got even better. In the revised edition of her autobiography, *Past Imperfect,* she rhapsodized, "We have been together now for a year and a half and even though I am wary of emotional involvement, Peter has been good for me." Then came a minicliff-hanger: "I would like to predict that Peter and I will live happily ever after as the storybook ends. But I realize there are no guarantees in life and the only constant is change."

Her prediction did not come true. And there would be no storybook ending. Their marriage would end in a divorce that rivaled any *Dynasty* plot for drama and flamboyance. What's more, it would be revealed during the trial that they had spent a good deal of time prior to the marriage arguing about a pre-nuptial agreement.

Yet some fruitful things were produced during their courtship and marriage, most noticeably the miniseries *Sins* and *Monte Carlo*. Together, Joan Collins and Peter Holm would work as executive producers, and Joan would also star in both productions. In *Sins* Joan deliberately chose a vehicle that would allow her to play a character unlike her *Dynasty* alter ego, Alexis. The character was a beautiful and powerful magazine magnate, Hélène Junot, who survived the Nazis during her childhood.

"I think it is very important for an actor not to be identified with one role on a weekly television series," Joan explains. "What happens is that when that series eventually ends, the public, as well as the directors, producers, and even network executives tend to think of the actor only as the character. As much as I have enjoyed playing Alexis, I have spent every hiatus getting away from her by playing somebody different like Hélène Junot."

It was a valuable experience for her in still another way. "Actors often have this thing about producers," she notes. "It's 'them against us.' I learned a tremendous amount while filming *Sins*. I have been in the business a long time, so I already knew quite a lot about the production side, but I have become infinitely more aware of the minutiae of the everyday life of a producer." Difficult as it was to wear two hats, Joan vows, "Now that I have done it, I don't think that I ever want to become involved with any new project unless it's my own."

Sins certainly turned out to be a much more successful project, in terms of Joan finally getting complete control of a project. She had wanted this for a long time, as far back as *The Stud,* which she had gotten an option on. "But then I was told by people that I couldn't produce and be in it, too," she recalls. "So, I—always playing the obedient dolt—handed over the production reins to various people, among them my ex-husband Ron Kass. But, at the same time, I realized that I had been marketed or exploited all my life."

Her then-fourth husband, Peter Holm, she said, fueled her entrepreneurial yearnings. As she told interviewers: "It was Peter who made me realize that I had the power or bankability to take control. He said I was sort of—how do you say it—'hot.'" At first Joan demurred, but then, recalling George Hamilton's immortal line, "Joan, better to be a shrewd businesswoman than a screwed actress," she cottoned to the idea.

Her reasoning: "Instead of being hired, or having somebody come to me and suggest that I do some television movie, I had a project of my own in which I could be involved in a more creative level." Joan also liked the notion of casting some of her friends in *Sins.* One friend, Timothy Dalton, played her brother, and disco doyenne Regine also had a part, as did Joan's secretary, and her daughter Katy. Song-and-dance man, Gene Kelly, a friend from her early Hollywood days, played one of her husbands. "The hardest part," Joan says, "was casting the young me." She chose Catherine Mary Stewart and was delighted by her performance. "A brave move," Joan says with a chuckle. "I took over at twenty-nine. But actually I believe I carried it off. I am very objective about myself. I had a wonderful, brilliant cameraman. I changed my voice and my walk and my attitude."

Her labor of love was also a division of labor. "We basically divided the things we were involved in fairly early down the middle," she says. "He

[Holm] was involved in all the money things, financing, contracts, and what I call the boring bits. We didn't touch base a lot. He felt there were things I was good at that he wasn't, and things that he was good at that I wasn't. It was pretty evenly matched." How much business experience Holm, whose real name is Peter Gustaf Sjoholm, had was somewhat dubious. He was variously described as an ex-pop star, in his native Sweden, and by Joan, once, as "in manufacturing."

The editor, Bob Tanner, of the updated version of Joan's autobiography, does not give Holm high marks as a businessman. "It was difficult to deal with him," Tanner says, "because he didn't understand publishing. And it was always 'Call Hollywood' to try to reach either of them." Some 110 extra pages, which he bought from Holm, were involved. "He thought he was acting as a blackmailer," Tanner adds. "He said that if we didn't pay what he was asking, then they would publish the book themselves. He failed to understand that because he did not own the rights to the book he could not do this."

Sins was shown on American television for three nights in a row. It is the story of Hélène Junot, a beautiful magazine publisher whose life at the top is quite complicated. On her way to the top she had made many enemies. Getting there, in the first place, had not been easy. As a Jewish child in Nazi-occupied France, she had witnessed many horrors, among them her mother being beaten and tortured by a Nazi.

Despite the sorrowful theme of Hélène's early years, the miniseries was an elaborate and expensive production. Some critics objected to so much glitz in a story that showed, in part, some of the horrors of the Holocaust.

Joan and Peter did not stint on anything. Valentino supplied no fewer than thirty-five outfits for Joan's character in the final episodes. All the settings, which Joan had been so keen on from the start, were filmed on location.

"I was not adverse to the idea of filming in Paris, Venice and the South of France," Joan remarked at the time. "Los Angeles is not my idea of glamour. I did not want to spend another summer filming in Southern California." Away from work, Joan and Peter would vacation in other sun spots like Acapulco and Antigua.

What attracted Joan to *Sins* was the power as much as the glamour of the story. "I just loved the book," Joan says. "It's a story with real scope. I was very interested in this woman's transformation from an innocent young girl into a high-powered executive."

While promoting the miniseries, Joan was asked by *People* magazine if she sinned in real life. True to her character she gave an honest answer. She began by defining sins as "murder, rape, brutality, violence, meanness, lying and hurting people," and then explained, "I think in terms of what *I* call 'sin,' I don't sin at all." And what of the punishment for those she considers to be sinners? "I think people get what they deserve in life," she stated. "Actually I really do. And I think you reap what you deserve. I think a lot of the time you get the fate you deserve. I certainly don't believe that life is totally fair."

On whether she believed in God, Joan, who once described herself as a semi-agnostic, said: "I don't know—I believe in a greater being of some kind."

She was asked if she felt there was a Heaven or a Hell. "Heaven, I honestly don't know," Joan replied. "Hell? No, I don't believe in it."

Incredibly, Joan, with her perfect figure that slithers into all her gorgeous designer gowns, confessed to the sin of gluttony. "Perhaps one day a month," she says, "I'm a chocoholic." Alcohol, she points out, is okay, but only in moderation. "I don't believe in getting drunk and driving," she says emphatically, adding that wine and champagne are her favorite choices. She swears off drugs, pills, or pot totally, and disdains any use of them.

Sins would test Joan and Peter as well. If their individual egos did not collide on a grand scale on this project, she reasoned, then probably they could make a marriage work. Between *Sins* and *Monte Carlo,* Joan would costar with Peter in another very important production, namely their marriage ceremony on November 3, 1985. Only this time the location was Las Vegas, in a small chapel with only seven guests and a minister in attendance. Sister Jackie skipped the event.

There were other no-shows among her friends, though, in fairness, the wedding ceremony was something of a secret until the last moment. "A disaster," one friend called the marriage. "None of us liked Holm. We told her. When he was around Joan, he wouldn't talk to anyone else but her. After a while she knew to book a table for two when she was meeting you for lunch. Joan realized that her friends would only see her without him around. But on the other hand, you never really know what goes on in a relationship between two people."

Said one friend who did attend: "Joan looked beautiful in an off-white evening gown with a low back while Peter wore a white tux with a pink tie." But, according to that same guest, both of them seemed very nervous. "There was a lot of stuttering in their voices, and tension, and a great deal of emotion," she added. "The ring was absolutely beautiful; it had four rows of diamonds. Both Peter and Joan were so relieved after the ceremony." The wedding cake was decorated with pink roses. And

Holm toasted the occasion with a glass of apple juice.

Holm then cut his first business deal as her husband. Syndicated columnist Cindy Adams reported: "Despite the hallowed moment when he and the bride exchanged their 'I Do's,' despite the ceremony's privileged specialness, Husband No. 4 managed to think clear-headedly enough to hustle the exclusive wedding photos." A supermarket tabloid got them. Joan remembers challenging her new husband about the pictures, but says he convinced her it was better for them to get the money than someone else.

Owing to the small ceremony, when the newlyweds arrived in London, they decided to stage another celebration for friends and family. A reluctant Joe Collins was among them, but Jackie abstained again. A quite lavish party was held at the fashionable Chelsea nightclub Stocks. The mood of the party was dampened slightly when Peter Holm tried to physically remove a top London journalist from the room. She had come along as a guest of someone else. While Peter pulled at her arms, the owner intervened on her behalf. He told Holm, in effect, that Stocks was his club, and the woman journalist was welcome to stay. The party resumed peacefully with an all-woman band performing and champagne flowing. But the papers were quick to pick up on the confrontation in days to follow.

There was no honeymoon. It was back to work for Joan. Her *Dynasty* schedule remained as hectic as ever and her public engagements just as demanding. Then, during her vacation from *Dynasty*, Joan began work on her next miniseries, *Monte Carlo*. Just like *Sins*, this production attracted an enormous amount of publicity.

One reason was that, not since her days with Newley, when she performed a song in his erotic musical comedy, had Joan sung publicly. In the lead role, this time as a Russian-born singer out to avenge the killing of her husband, Joan is a spy who seduces enemy generals into revealing war secrets. Between her connivances, Joan crooned, "The Last Time I Saw Paris."

The success that characterized their miniseries did not seem to extend to their marriage. Reports of marital discord were beginning to surface, along with antics like their checking in at Charles de Gaulle airport outside Paris with forty-nine pieces of luggage. Soon their high-flying life, said to include chartered flights between Paris and Nice, would come to a dramatic halt.

In December 1986, only eleven months after their wedding, Joan filed for divorce. When someone rang Joan's father to report what he called bad news, the late Joe Collins said: "Call that bad news? It's the best news I've had all year." From Joan's point of view, the couple had a pre-nuptial agreement and, further, Holm had already gotten everything that was promised to him. That, according to Joan, added up to a grand total of over one million dollars. She added that because of her past history, with at least one of her husbands, Reed, demanding money, she had made a pre-nuptial agreement a condition of marrying Holm in the first place. Especially now that she was a woman of more than considerable means, such an agreement was crucial to her survival.

Holm's reaction was more spontaneous. "Everything was lovey-dovey," he said, then admitted, "We'd had a few arguments. We agreed to meet for lunch and talk things over. Instead, someone from her attorney's office showed up at the restaurant and handed me something he said was the divorce papers. I was stunned and flabbergasted."

It was, no doubt, in that same state of shock that

he called a locksmith to change the locks on Joan's Beverly Hills house. Holm then barred anyone from entering. Clearly, he did not see the pre-nuptial agreement in quite the same way as Joan, or, in the end, as the judge who heard the case. He took a much more relaxed view of the pre-nuptial agreement than his ex-wife-to-be. In his opinion, it was just an agreement between them, without any legal implications and done merely to appease Joan who would not marry him without the document.

The dispute ended up in court and became a hit show rivaled only by *Dynasty Divorce Court* and *The Price Is Right* all rolled into one. Headlines around the world came up with other descriptions, "Cash 'n' Chaos" and "Divorcing for Dollars," among them, to describe the event. Fox Television's *A Current Affair* even ran a mock telethon to raise funds for Peter Holm, though in the end its host, Maury Povich, told the defendant Holm, simply, "Peter, get a job."

At issue was Holm's demand for half of Joan's earnings, which his lawyer figured to be between four and five million dollars during the period of their marriage, under California's community property law. Additionally, until the court issued a decision, Holm wanted temporary alimony of around eighty thousand dollars per month.

Presumably, at forty-one, Holm was able-bodied enough to earn his own money. Certainly if anyone gave proof to this notion it was Joan, at fifty-four, with her almost bionic energy and zeal for work. His problem, however, was altogether different. It was, simply, how to maintain the life-style to which he had become accustomed during the marriage.

And what, exactly, was that life-style? By Holm's calculation, which he presented in court, he needed the following per month: rent, $16,500;

household salaries, $7,000; groceries, $1900; telephone, $1300; TV/video, $670; audio supplies, $400; lease of a BMW auto, $3910; personal grooming, $200; clothing and accessories, $12,000; entertainment, $6,000; travel, $4,000. Other incidentals included $500 in limousine services and $8,000 for a curious category called "cash draws spent on personal items and purchases." Owing to the fact that these figures were based on the calendar year 1986, he added, the monthly total "may have increased due to inflation." The case came to trial in 1987.

Joan, meanwhile, asked nothing more of Holm than to regain her freedom. She charged there had been some mismanagement of their finances. Collins also accused Holm of trying to come between her and her children. As a result, she said, she got heart palpitations and had to consult a doctor.

The courtroom bickerings attracted worldwide press attention, including half of Fleet Street. As one publication put it: "The show playing Monday through Thursday (possibly Friday) of this week at the Los Angeles courtroom stars *Dynasty*'s Joan Collins and her estranged husband Peter Holm. Also featured in roles are renowned divorce lawyer Marvin Mitchelson, representing Collins, and Holm's attorney, Frank Steinschriber." One report pointed out the irony of Joan declaring, "I've been taken advantage of by men since I was 20," while another called Holm, "This shameless Swede asking his wife of eleven months for $2.6 million and calling her 'the woman I love.'"

Just as in all great Hollywood productions, there was, of course, a surprise witness—the other woman—direct from central casting. She was Romina Danielson, twenty-three, a bronzed bombshell who had been married to a friend of Holm. The nickname given her by Holm, she said, was "Passion Flower." Romina testified on the stand

that she had been Holm's lover during his marriage to Collins, and also, that they had hatched a
scheme whereby Peter would remain with Joan for
a period long enough to legally claim half her assets. Ten minutes into her astonishing revelations,
Joan Collins stormed out of the courtroom.
Romina also mentioned a time when she thought
she might be pregnant from sex with Holm. Then,
as if almost perfectly on cue, Romina Danielson
fainted and paramedics carried her away.

Joan also had her moment on the witness stand.
As *The Washington Post*'s Cynthia Gorney wrote:
"It was hard not to fixate on her lips. She had these
amazing lips, sort of full and constantly at work
there below the smoke-colored eyelids and the
large tousled hair. The hair was mesmerizing too,
especially on Wednesday when a single velvet bow
appeared to be perilously containing the whole ar-
rangement, and when she walked back into the
courtroom after lunch she had a peach-colored
rose in one hand and the black velvet bow in the
back—and she would lift the rose to her face, you
see, as though preparing to kiss it—Anyway, the
lips. These lips are worth $95,000 per episode,
which is what Collins testified she made last season
on 'Dynasty.' These lips pouted and pursed, and
made small moves in the general direction of the
press corps, which was dutifully taking notes."

A day after Holm's "Passion Flower" wilted on
the stand, the hearing was over. Despite the
tongue-in-cheek media coverage, from Joan's point
of view the event was a quite serious matter. In the
end the public was won over to Joan's side, and
apparently the judge shared their view. Holm
agreed to accept a reported $180,000 and a $40,000
custom-built sports car, a pittance compared with
the $2.6 million and $80,000-a-month temporary
alimony sought by him.

Joan Collins, however, had cause for celebration. She shared the evening with close friends including Angie Dickinson and Jacqueline Bisset. Someone presented Joan with a T-shirt that had "I Am Holmless" on it.

Holm, meanwhile, apparently started thinking about his livelihood. Possibly inspired by the success of his ex-sister-in-law, Jackie Collins the author, Holm looked into this field. Perhaps there might be a publisher, he reasoned, who would want a book about his side of the story. Holm would engage New York literary and screen agent Joseph Singer who discovered his new client on the Phil Donahue Show. Of Holm's publishing prospects, agent Singer said at the time, "I don't think it will be much of a problem. Their romance is a great story. Peter still has feelings for Joan. Their relationship is very special to him. He wants to write an honest book."

After meeting with Holm and signing him up, Singer declared, "Holm has a great business head. You get a feeling he knows what he's doing." He added, "Six publishing houses have expressed interest in the Holm book."

But Joan's own literary agent, Irving "Swifty" Lazar, quickly offered his own assessment: "There is no audience for that book and a legitimate publisher wouldn't take it."

Lazar's opinion apparently prevailed over that of Singer. To date there is still no Holm book. Joan, however, did not lose any sleep over Holm's attempt to cash in on Collins. As she remarked in a London press conference, "How can he write a book—he can barely write his name." At the same time Joan admitted, "I don't think anyone would like to have the person that you've been the closest to in three and a half years write all the most intimate details of your life."

Looking back on the Holm chapter of her life, Joan admits to being left with feelings of both pain and anger. As she told talk show host Oprah Winfrey in October 1988: "It was so ridiculous, it was so embarrassing that all I could do was just pretend it wasn't happening. I just sort of put myself into another space somehow or another. I tried to do a lot of mental relaxation because I thought otherwise I'll go completely mad. I was in that courtroom for over six days for eight hours a day and it was one of those things when you are really washing your dirty linen in public."

Joan Collins, though, would have little to fear. With her popularity from *Dynasty* and outside charitable acts, she had the public well and truly in her corner.

Post Holm

Despite Peter Holm's unsuccessful attempts to tell all, Joan Collins's next boyfriend, Bill Wiggins, not only managed to get his story published, but also to remain pals with Joan. The British property dealer, nicknamed Bungalow Bill by the press, who claims his assets reside more in the lower than upper region of his body, told all in a serialization in the *Sun* newspaper. But wanting to write stories about life with Joan Collins seemed about all Bill Wiggins had in common with Peter Holm.

It was at a friend's lunch that Bill Wiggins met the woman who would put him in the British headlines. He was invited on the premise of being introduced to a blond bombshell. As a measure of his self-assurance, perhaps, he turned up forty minutes late. It was then that he realized the mention of a mystery woman was just a ploy to lure him to the lunch. However, he was not at all disappointed to discover that the so-called blond bombshell was, in fact, a beautiful brunette, namely Joan Collins.

For once the cool bachelor was caught off guard and left somewhat speechless. He quickly found the appropriate words: "So sorry, I didn't catch your name." It worked on Joan, a woman who has probably heard every line in the book. The *Dynasty* star, he remembers, laughed at his line.

Joan herself is known to possess a sense of humor. As she told one interviewer who commented on her fresh appearance after a transatlantic flight:

"The pilot asked me the same thing. 'I want to know your secret. Don't you suffer from jet lag?' And I said no. And he said, 'I must do what you do. What is it you do?' I said, 'I sleep on the plane.' He said, 'Oh, I don't think *I* can do that.' " Wiggins also finds her witty. "There is nothing aloof or Alexis about her," he told the *Sun*. "Joan is the funniest woman I have ever met." As it turned out, it was his own sense of humor that captivated Joan. A privately educated man in his forties with a smooth, husky voice and classical-style clothes, Wiggins is an English gent with what he described to the *Sun* as "the classic British ability to laugh at myself," adding, "And so has Joan. We're always taking the mickey out of one another."

Delighted with Joan, he had no idea whether there would be another opportunity to see her again. "I knew I liked her and there was an attraction," he confessed in the same newspaper, "but she was a busy woman." As luck would have it, Wiggins's presence as an extra man was in demand at a dinner party to which Joan had also been invited. They spent most of the night locked in conversation. After the party they dropped by Wiggins's house. There, Wiggins told the *Sun*, he was struck by an irony: " 'God, Joan,' I said, 'I just realized your fur coat probably costs more than this entire house.' "

Joan, according to Bill, fixed their next date. From then on Bill Wiggins and Joan Collins were seen in each other's company regularly. In May 1987, Joan even dropped in at a celebrity golf tournament in the British Midlands to watch Wiggins play the last few holes. Swooping down on the eighteenth hole in a helicopter, Joan brought play to a halt momentarily when she alighted from it. Then, walking along the soft grounds of the fairway in high heels, she cheered Wiggins on, applauding for good drives and taking pictures of him. Another *Dynasty* star, Diahann Carroll, also on the scene to root for her husband Vic Damone, told the Associated Press at the time that she and Joan were taking golf lessons together.

Bill, however, made it clear from the opening round of their relationship that he had no intention of becoming Husband No. 5, and furthermore, intended to remain close to some of his ex-girlfriends. Joan's response to all this, according to Bill, was the opposite of what Alexis might have pulled under similar circumstances. "She doesn't storm off in a rage when I talk to a woman," he explained in the *Sun* serialization, "and she isn't a bitch about them. Joan never tries to cut them down or ignore them. Joan is a lovely warm woman." He added, however, that he could understand why such a "highly successful, attractive woman" as Joan could intimidate other females.

At that point Joan was quite gun-shy herself about marriage. Almost two years after her divorce, in October 1988 she still felt that way. Asked by an interviewer then if she had any plans to marry again, Joan replied, "No, I don't see that there's any reason or necessity to get married again. I mean, I think I've done it. I don't think you get married unless you really like the state of being married, the state of living with somebody, which I do. But since it seems it hasn't worked out very well for me, I'd be too terrified that it wouldn't work again."

Wiggins also found himself as wary about the Holm entanglement as Joan. "When people see me with Joan," he told the *Sun*, "I have this awful fear that they think, 'Oh, there goes another Peter Holm.'" The reason he gave the *Sun* interview, he said, was to dispel any notions that he might be the sequel to Peter Holm. "I have never met the man and have no wish to," Wiggins declared in the same piece. "From what I gather, Peter wasn't able to join in and have a laugh. That must have been a recipe for disaster because the way to turn Joan Collins on is to make her laugh."

Wiggins said that he got to meet a stellar cast of Joan's Hollywood friends including several *Dynasty* members, as well as Elizabeth Taylor, George Segal, fellow Brits Roger Moore and Michael Caine and their wives and, of course, Joan's sister, Jackie Collins, and her husband. "I made a point of not being just a hanger-on," Wiggins stated firmly in the *Sun.* "I am anything but a kept man. Joan does not pay for me to fly all over the world or lavish me with gifts." One present that she did give him was a T-shirt printed with the words, "Men of Kent Do It Better" on it, an apparent reference to the county where Wiggins grew up. Today Wiggins, a successful property dealer, lives in the fashionable Chelsea district of London and drives a Porsche. He is irked by the nickname, Buffalo Bill, that the London press pinned on him. As he told the *Sun,* "I really resent people thinking I'm thick. It's certainly not fair. I am certainly not stupid. Winston Churchill wasn't very academic and he didn't do badly."

Nor has the resolute bachelor Bill Wiggins. In capturing the attention of Joan Collins, of whom Dean Martin once said, "Every guy in America would like to date," Bill Wiggins became for a time the envy of millions of males all over the world.

Since their widely reported friendship, Joan has also been seen in the company of other men, including Bill's friend and real-estate colleague Malcolm Fraser. For the moment, at least, such relationships suit a somewhat marriage-shy Joan Collins just fine.

Futures

In what may be construed as sibling rivalry, Joan has made a foray into Jackie's field by writing a potboiler novel called *Prime Time*. Upon its release, the book went straight onto the best-seller lists in America and England, and got mixed reviews. Writing it, Joan says, allowed her to be creative all on her own as opposed to just being part of a collaborative effort. "When you are an actress, you have dozens of other people that are involved, and you're just one tiny cog in a whole group of things," Joan explains. "When you are writing, it's just you and a yellow pad, so when it comes out, when you do it, it's like your baby, the thing you've been carrying inside your head for the past two or three or four years, however long it takes you to do it. So it's creatively the thing that has made me feel the most fulfilled."

The notion that she could write a novel and that it could be better than some other popular novels struck her while on a skiing holiday with family and friends about four years ago. She was inspired by some of the boring novels she took along on holiday as much as by all she had observed on *Dynasty*. "Eventually, I thought, I can write a better novel," she revealed to Oprah Winfrey. "And so I started writing in that ten days that I had left and by the end of the ten days, I had 10,000 words. And I found it much more interesting to write at that particular time than to read."

At the time of *Prime Time*'s publication, the theme of sibling rivalry was dredged up once again by interviewers. Joan was quick to point out that many brothers and sisters enter the same professions; she admitted, though, that prior to writing her first novel, she had a few reservations of her own. She remembers: "First of all I thought about it a lot. I thought, well, Jackie is one of the most famous novelists in the world, and one of the most successful, and I love her books and I think they're wonderful, and how is she going to feel if I do this? And then I thought, well, she is so successful—she is right at the top of the heap—that how can she really possibly mind, because it's like saying to Jeff Bridges, 'Well, you can't be an actor because Beau Bridges is an actor, too, and your father, Lloyd Bridges, is an actor.' Just because people are in the same family, I don't think it should preclude you from doing something, if you feel you've got it in you."

Jackie herself did not appear to think Joan was invading her turf. Instead she seemed, publicly at least, to applaud Joan's latest venture. "It's great," Jackie told one talk-show host while promoting her twelfth novel some months before the publication of Joan's first. But then she stopped short at appraising her sister's talent as a fiction writer. "I've no idea what it's like," she said. "I'm going to discover this along with everyone else."

How, the interviewer pressed, did Jackie truly *feel* about Joan's debut as a novelist? "I'm fine about it," she said tersely. "Joan is an actress, and I'm sure everybody perceives her as such, and so do I." Then, somewhat gratuitously, Jackie remarked, "I think it's great. If somebody's got the courage to sit down and write their first novel, good luck to them. Everyone should try to write one."

Not everyone, of course, can be as prolific as Jackie Collins. With twelve novels to her credit already, she is alreading planning the next one. Though the number thirteen may strike some superstitious people as a bad omen, with Jackie Collins's track record at the bookstore and her pluck, the next one should come up a big winner, too.

What, her public wonders, will be the next theme of this best-selling novelist? Certainly she has more than captured all the twists in the lives of Hollywood wives, husbands, and even rock stars. "I'm going to write a book called *Lady Boss*," says Jackie, quite appropriately since she has something of a mini-empire going herself. "It's a sequel to two books I wrote before called *Lucky* and *Chances*, and it's about a strong woman who goes in and takes over Hollywood." Though it may seem that Jackie already wrote the last word on Hollywood, incredibly, she suggests there is more fertile ground to mine. "I like going back to Hollywood for books," she explains, "because it's an interesting community to write about and there's so much going on there."

With all her millions, of course, Jackie could retire her pen for the rest of her life. But she assures her millions of fans that she intends to keep writing. "I think when you really want to tell stories," she says, "you do it because you love to do it. And I love what I do. I've never done it for the money."

There is more—besides novels—to come. Jackie also aims to direct films. "At the moment *Hollywood Husbands* is being written as a screenplay," she says. "I'm the executive producer, and I want to make it hot, interesting, and funny."

There are also rumors of a novel by Jackie about Hollywood kids in the making. A big question also remains about whether there will be a sequel to *Rock Star*. The author herself shares the same curiosity about this as her readers. "A lot of people who bought the book are asking me, 'But what happens next?' " she claims, adding, "*I* don't know. Maybe I will sometime in the future because I want to know what happens to Kris Phoenix . . . so, maybe."

For the more immediate future, Kris Phoenix may be turning up on the silver screen. Reportedly, Jackie has sold the film rights to *Rock Star* and also plans to sign on as an executive producer. Already she has some casting ideas. "I would really love Whitney Houston to play Rafealla," Jackie says, referring to the exotically beautiful mulatto chanteuse in the book. "This is not a firm offer, but it's going to be made into a movie, and I think she would be great in the part."

Willing talk-show guest that Jackie is, she has also been wooed with offers to step around the other side of the desk to host her own American television series. To date, her answer has been a firm no. "What with my writing, my family, my three big dogs, and even my social life," she gasps, "I'm busy enough."

Her fortunes have not relieved her, however, of one frustration. "Even if I became President of the United States," Jackie has been quoted as saying, "in England I will always be known as Joan Collins's little sister."

This quote strikes most people as untrue. With more than seventy million copies of Jackie's books in over thirty countries, she is one of the most famous writers in the world. She not only has, as one observer put it, film-star status, but is also the first to know what happens in the fast lanes of Hollywood Hills. Though there have been many imitators, Jackie Collins is the original act, and the only one to keep coming around the bend time and time again with still another best-seller.

As for her staying power, Jackie says that she expects to live until she is at least eighty-five. "I will continue to be eccentric and canny, too," she vows. "I'll invite all my relatives in, videotape them, secretly study the tapes, and figure out which ones want the money. Then I'll give it to the one who doesn't want anything."

Hollywood wives and husbands, though, had better not lay their worries to rest. Jackie promises to reveal all their names after her death. "I'll leave the real names to be read," she vows, "in a little black box." And where might it be? Jackie is mum. A possible place might be London. "I know *I'll* go back to Britain," she says. "Although I love being in America, I'm intrinsically British."

Jackie's older and budding-novelist sister Joan Collins also approaches her future with a touch of humor. "I have to admit," she comments, "that I'm not looking forward to death." But when the final curtain comes down, says the woman who manages to look voluptuous and also stay svelte, she wants, "She had her cake and ate it, too," on her gravestone.

For now, of course, Joan Collins believes she has still a lot of living and working, as always, to do. Though in doubt in her own mind about how much longevity she wants on *Dynasty*, Joan went full-speed ahead on the talk-show circuit to promote her first novel, *Prime Time*. In the past, Joan had two best-sellers, the *Joan Collins Beauty Book* and her tell-all autobiography, *Past Imperfect*. Now she has a third with her novel, and has proved that her imagination can be as salable and even salacious as some of her facts. *Prime Time*, according to Joan, was just her opening act on what was heretofore more Jackie's stage.

Indeed, Joan also foresees other roles for herself on both the stage and screen. Ever since *Rally*

Round the Flag, Boys in her early Hollywood days, Joan has always fancied the part of a comedienne. With her gift of humor, that should hardly be difficult to achieve.

The type of serious role Joan would like to do would be of a woman like Maria Callas. "She (Callas) was a prima donna, grand diva, tremendous jet-set star," Joan once said. "But underneath it all, she was just a woman in love who was being crushed and destroyed by this man. And she was a victim. I don't usually like to play women who are victims. But I thought that I could maybe have been like that, because I did have a tendency to throw it all over for love." Her first feature film in years, *Capri Numbers*, filmed in Europe in the summer of 1988, will soon grace the silver screen with Joan as both executive producer and star.

Theater, says Joan, is something she also intends to do again. "I'd love to do Tennessee Williams's *Streetcar*," she says, "but I feel I'm not Robert De Niro, who is, you know, one hundred percent dedicated to his craft, and lives, breathes, eats acting. I'm one hundred percent dedicated to my life and the enjoyment of it."

Her locale of choice in later life will certainly be Europe, either at home in London or at her villa in the South of France. Unlike Jackie, who intends only to wind up her days in Britain, Joan can hardly wait to move back to England. To this end, in 1988, Joan Collins also became a landlady, renting her Beverly Hills home for a reported twenty thousand dollars a week to Aussie Paul Hogan. While he was wrapping up *Crocodile Dundee II* in Hollywood, Joan was off working in Europe. Summer in Los Angeles is not, if she can help it, in her future.

Not one to shed crocodile or any other tears over past amours or husbands, Joan intends to walk into her next marriage, should there be one at all, with her eyes wide open this time. For the immediate future, Joan says, her three children are comforting and company enough. "Though I've had to deal with a lot of rejection in my career," she says, "it was lucky, because I had the time to bring up my wonderful children. I've always been very lucky to be very healthy and I've always had a lot of joie de vivre." As it is, she travels at least fourteen times a year, often over a weekend, to be near her youngest daughter, who is in day school in Europe.

Adds the woman, who posed, at fifty, for *Playboy:* "We're not like our mothers and grandmothers, who were worn out by childbearing and housekeeping." Joan also believes she has good genes. "My grandmother lived to ninety," says Joan, adding, "I'll settle for one hundred."

Because Gemini Joan and her sister Jackie are such stellar talents, we asked an internationally known astrologer and author of *Secrets from a Star Gazer's Notebook*, Debbi Kempton-Smith, to read the futures of both. Here are just a few of her predictions: "Jackie's Libra luck is found in Joan's sign of Gemini. Joan has been very lucky for Jackie in a kind of karmic way. All of 1989 will bring Jackie a great deal of luck, especially with her books. She's going to make a lot of money and have a lot of good times. Joan has now had most of her pain, and she's really paid, and she will make a wonderful life with someone, maybe a surgeon, of her caliber."

The astrologer finds a great humanity in both sisters. Incredibly, of the woman who gets megabucks for her raunchy books, Kempton-Smith says, "Jackie may have been in a former life a nun who made a vow with poverty and gave all her possessions away. In this life there may be a certain amount of guilt that has been carried over from her past life." And speaking of vows, the astrologer also notes, "Jackie is a very loyal person. When she makes a promise she keeps it. She would rather die than break a lunch date with a friend. In fact, she would have to be dying for her *not* to make it."

As for Joan, who by her own admission does not much care for celibacy, the astrologer sees in her future some noble mission. "There will be a bit of Bob Geldof (the 'Band-Aid' organizer) coming out in her. I have a feeling that Joan will receive a calling for some relief work. Interestingly, if Joan had not become an actress, she would have become a doctor. Although she doesn't like blood, she loves helping people. She has a touch with people, and they love to be around her. She has never yet found a group of people with charisma to equal her own. People usually don't become cosmic because they're having a bubble bath, but instead because they've watched their husband turn out to be a gold digger. But the hell and humiliation she went through with Holm is over. Because she did nothing to bring on the hurt and betrayal, a scar remains and will never go away. This is a highly sensitive woman."

Irene Kassorla, an internationally known psychologist, lecturer and author of *Go For It!,* recommends: "Joan should definitely stick to her own kind. Someone from Buckingham Palace should not marry someone from Brooklyn. Preferably, the man should be somebody outside of show business, closer in age, and who shares the same esteem in the community in terms of social and economic status."

Whatever man Joan chooses or manuscript Jackie creates, they are destined to remain in the limelight and continue their own inimitable saga as the Hollywood Sisters.